W9-AZF-077

TRUMP-STYLE NEGOTIATION

Powerful Strategies and Tactics for Mastering Every Deal

GEORGE H. ROSS

WILEY

JOHN WILEY & SONS, INC.

Copyright © 2006 by George H. Ross. All rights reserved.

Published by John Wiley & Sons, Inc., Hoboken, New Jersey.
Published simultaneously in Canada.

No part of this publication may be reproduced, stored in a retrieval system, or transmitted in any form or by any means, electronic, mechanical, photocopying, recording, scanning, or otherwise, except as permitted under Section 107 or 108 of the 1976 United States Copyright Act, without either the prior written permission of the Publisher, or authorization through payment of the appropriate per-copy fee to the Copyright Clearance Center, Inc., 222 Rosewood Drive, Danvers, MA 01923, (978) 750-8400, fax (978) 646-8600, or on the web at www.copyright.com. Requests to the Publisher for permission should be addressed to the Permissions Department, John Wiley & Sons, Inc., 111 River Street, Hoboken, NJ 07030, (201) 748-6011, fax (201) 748-6008, or online at http://www.wiley.com/go/permissions.

Limit of Liability/Disclaimer of Warranty: While the publisher and author have used their best efforts in preparing this book, they make no representations or warranties with respect to the accuracy or completeness of the contents of this book and specifically disclaim any implied warranties of merchantability or fitness for a particular purpose. No warranty may be created or extended by sales representatives or written sales materials. The advice and strategies contained herein may not be suitable for your situation. You should consult with a professional where appropriate. Neither the publisher nor author shall be liable for any loss of profit or any other commercial damages, including but not limited to special, incidental, consequential, or other damages.

For general information on our other products and services or for technical support, please contact our Customer Care Department within the United States at (800) 762-2974, outside the United States at (317) 572-3993 or fax (317) 572-4002.

Wiley also publishes its books in a variety of electronic formats. Some content that appears in print may not be available in electronic books. For more information about Wiley products, visit our web site at www.wiley.com.

ISBN-13: 978-0-470-04586-2

ISBN-10: 0-470-04586-8

Printed in the United States of America.

10 9 8 7 6 5 4 3 2

To my wonderful wife Billie
who has always been and
will always be the wind beneath my wings.

Contents

CONTENTS

CONTENTS

FOREWORD

THE FIRST TIME I met George Ross was in the 1970s. I was 27 years old and I was involved with my very first real estate foray, my adventure into Manhattan.

At the time, George was the senior partner in a major New York law firm dealing in real estate. George immediately understood the complexities of the deal I was trying to negotiate. This impressed me because no one had ever done that type of deal before. I had to negotiate major concessions from many different parties to make it work.

It was a complicated hotel deal—a bankrupt railroad-owned property next to Grand Central Terminal in New York, that I ended up turning into the Grand Hyatt. I had to work with a railroad, the city of New York, and the state government and the banks and a large number of other parties—none of whom thought it would work. George had no direct experience in some of these areas but even so, he seemed to know exactly how to put the whole thing together to match my vision. I needed the deal to specify that I would pay no property taxes or rent (except a share of the profits). At that time in the 1970s, however, the city was approaching bankruptcy—foreclosures were rampant—so to create and operate a first class hotel from a building that was totally decrepit was a challenge, to say the least. In fact, the whole thing took two years of constant negotiations to put together. Without George's negotiating expertise, the deal would have failed many times over. Instead, it was so successful it launched my career.

I like to think of myself as a maverick, someone who's willing to do something that no one else is willing to do. But as I learned during that two years, having a vision isn't enough; you also need an expert advisor—someone who understands your ideas well enough to carry them forward, but who is also shrewd enough to negotiate on your behalf. George is a top real estate lawyer but more important (and this is unusual for a lawyer), he is also a shrewd businessman and negotiator. That combination was the key.

I like to work in broad strokes, deal with the big picture, but not the details. For the details, I rely almost entirely on George. He is able to put my vision into concrete terms, but he is also a natural at judging how any given negotiation needs to proceed; what the other side wants and needs; and how to get results. You are very fortunate to have this book and to be getting the same negotiation wisdom for which I paid George extremely well!

DONALD J. TRUMP

INTRODUCTION

How I Became Donald Trump's Negotiator

Over the past 30 years of working with Donald Trump, I've come to learn the key element in his business style: He is a genius at establishing a relationship with the other party. He understands the human element. My role has been to negotiate the transaction; that's my strength. It's Trump's vision, but I handle the details. This has worked well for us.

Although co-starring on *The Apprentice* is what I am now best known for, for many years I have worked with Donald, as advisor, negotiator, and attorney. I have watched him in action as he structured and completed major transactions, and I helped him negotiate many of the biggest real estate deals imaginable, including Trump Tower, the GM Building, the Grand Hyatt, and 40 Wall Street. As you might imagine, I gained a great deal of negotiating experience during this time. This came on top of my previous 30 years of experience negotiating major real estate deals, including the Chrysler Building and the St. Regis Hotel, for other developers.

Donald and I have worked out a fairly simple way of taking care of business. Once he realized, during our first collaborative real estate effort, that I would always finish my part of his deal, he let me handle another one. The way we work is that if and when I need him to intervene (usually when his personal relationship skills can be used to convince someone that he or she ought to go along with what we have in mind), he steps in. Otherwise, Donald gives me the freedom to handle the deal as I see fit, which places me in a unique position. I am able to do the legal work *and* the business negotiation at the same time. This is very unusual for any lawyer unless he also has considerable direct business experience, which most lawyers do not. We've use this efficient approach consistently, even when we have help from outside attorneys, which is often.

WHAT IS TRUMP-STYLE NEGOTIATION?

In this book, I am going to share with you many of the negotiating tactics and methods that I've developed over my 50 years of negotiating experience. I call these the *Trump style* of negotiation because they involve many of Trump's strategies. But I have also included many great lessons I learned from other New York real estate moguls I represented—or sat across the table from. These strategies work for many kinds of deals—buying a car, getting a raise from your boss, buying or selling a small investment property, or financing a skyscraper.

A big part of Trump's style involves playing up your strengths and delegating your weak points. He has an amazingly organized mind and he can solve problems, even complex ones, with remarkably creative solutions most other people wouldn't think of. He also understands how to figure out what the other side needs and wants, and he can see his way to the end result. So his vision and organization are the keys to his success. At the same time, he is not a detail-oriented person. He doesn't want to spend three days reading a lengthy lease one paragraph at a time. This is where I come into the picture. Trump-style negotiation involves the specific strategies I'm going to share with you. But you also have to know when to delegate and when to let experts step in and help you.

My Education in the Art of Negotiation

In the first three years of my legal career, I became something of a technician and expert in real estate law. I became adept at drafting contracts and all sorts of other documents. One of the things we'll talk about in this book is the great advantage of having all of the forms and legal documents in hand before you go into a negotiation, even if you have to draft them yourself. The existence of a form or contract makes it the "official" version—even when there isn't any such thing. Preparing any document in a negotiation gives you a great psychological edge because it is more difficult for the other side to propose a change once the form exists.

Before joining Trump, I was working as a real estate lawyer and having a lot of success. Finally, I went to my boss and said I wanted to be made a partner in the firm. He told me, "We don't make partners." So I left (but on good terms). From 1956 to 1966, I worked for Sol Goldman and Alex DiLorenzo Jr., who were becoming the biggest real estate investors in New York City, and I arranged for the purchase of 702 properties for these clients. That is more than one per week, each week, over a 10-year period. When you do that many deals, you learn just about every negotiation trick in the book, and you learn to predict how people are likely to react in every imaginable negotiating situation.

I had wide latitude for changing the terms of any deal. I was very young when I started, and I soon realized I was leaving a lot of my boss's money on the table. So, I began to carefully study the tactics of the other side in these deals, and I became very adept at negotiating.

Many years before meeting Donald Trump, I learned something else that is very important about negotiation: Not everyone tells the truth. Big surprise? Hardly. People are not going to employ the truth in a negotiation if it is to their advantage not to be totally truthful. This realization became a guiding principle in all of my negotiations: Always be nice, but stay skeptical. Forget what they tell me. Forget what they write me. What they are really trying to do is to get the numbers they want in a deal.

Some people will say anything if they think it will convince you. To become a skilled negotiator, you have to examine a transaction closely, listen intently to the other side, and see whether or not the words you hear match the real agenda that you suspect. Start negotiating from there and ask indirect as well as direct probing questions to pin down what the other side really wants.

I learned a lot from this simple but important fact of life. I've sat across the table from the prime players in real estate—people with huge, huge reputations, and I have found myself thinking, "If this guy can be such a snake, what are the rest of them up to?"

For example, I once negotiated something with a real estate executive, and he had his secretary type up the contract. I requested a few changes to which he agreed. But when the papers came back, I saw that the terms were not what we dictated. I had to go back and ask the guy across the desk, "Do you really want to close this deal?"

He said yes, so I responded, "Then bring your secretary in here with us. She types in front of me after we discuss what the papers are going to say. If you don't want to do that, then I won't do the deal."

This kind of confrontation was necessary, and it was an eye-opener to me that somebody with a big reputation would actually alter documents. I realized that I simply couldn't trust the guy. This was a tough lesson to learn at the beginning of my career, but it forced me to think about the whole negotiation process. People *will* change things, make promises, and play underhanded with you. You have to watch out for it because, unfortunately, it's all part of the process.

I learned a lot about negotiating before meeting Donald Trump, but even though I was toughened up by my own experience, Donald's style and creativity—his way of approaching business deals—led me in a completely different direction. When I first met Donald Trump in 1974, it was at a time when he had no track record in real estate. He was only 27 at the time and I was senior partner at Dreyer and Traub. Donald visited me on a referral from his father, Fred Trump, and frankly, I only saw Donald as a courtesy to his father. Donald was excited about the idea of buying and renovating the Commodore Hotel on 42nd Street in New York. He had an intricate plan for this run-down building next to Grand Central Terminal. It looked hopeless. Getting it to work would involve negotiating with railroad executives, the city of New York and its various agencies, state officials, and finding a willing lender—all of this by a young man with no experience. I cannot imagine a more difficult first project, but he was tenacious. He *knew* he could make it work. His confidence, passion, patience, vision, and ability to bring the parties together at the table, defined Trump-style negotiation as I practice it today.

After the Commodore Hotel purchase, I helped Donald on and off over the years. Eventually, he asked me to come work for him full-time, promising that he had many exciting and fun projects. Even with my many years of experience, I knew there was more to learn, so how could I resist such an offer? Donald Trump has given me tremendous freedom to operate in my own style. He has never questioned my reasons for making a decision or second-guessed anything I've done for him. He trusts me completely. Perhaps our track record together is one reason for this trust.

For example, when I came to work full-time for the Trump organization, 40 Wall Street was a one million square foot building that was nearly completely vacant, worth only about $1 million. Trump wanted to buy it, but the deal had numerous problems that seemed impossible to resolve. One thing Trump cannot bear is deadlock; he hates having deals drag on indefinitely. (Of course, this is a potential weakness and if someone on the other side knows this, he or she might be able to get a better deal just for speeding things up.) But Trump is smart, too. So he decided the only way to make 40 Wall Street work was to bring in expert help. He hired me with the mandate to get rid of the roadblocks and finalize the deal. After he conducted some brilliant negotiations with the owner, I advised him on how to make 40 Wall Street a financial success, and he gave me primary responsibility for managing and leasing it. Today, it is a successful office building worth more than $350 million.

One thing I learned from Donald is that negotiation is not always obvious or simple. At times, people say they want one thing, but what they say may exist primarily to serve a different purpose. In fact, that very idea—*you negotiate for one thing that exists primarily to serve a different purpose*—forms one of the bases of the whole Trump style of negotiation. For example, sometimes, publicity is more important than short-term profits, because that visibility opens up so many long-term doors. This is the Trump vision, the "bigger picture" that makes the difference between ordinary success and spectacular success.

If nothing else, when you're negotiating with anyone, you need to think strategically. What do you say you want and what do you really want? Ask the same question about the other side—once you know the answers, you're way ahead of most people, especially the people sitting across the table from you.

THE ORIGIN OF THIS BOOK

For more than 20 years, I have been a professor at New York University's School of Continuing Education and Professional Studies. Originally, I confined my lectures to real estate subjects based on my extensive experience. Although I had expertise in negotiation, I never considered the possibility of creating a college-level course on that subject. However, a number of years ago, at the end of a 16-hour real estate course, I had 15 minutes left over. For those students who were interested, I decided to share some thoughts on negotiation. In the written evaluation of my course, the students said that they found the 15 minutes on negotiation more helpful than the 16 hours of solving complex real estate problems.

Based on their feedback, I added 45 minutes of negotiation training at the end of my next lecture. Although the attendance was completely voluntary, no one left the room before the 45 minutes were up. The feedback was even more enthusiastic and many asked, "Why doesn't NYU have a course on negotiation?" At the urging of the program directors, I crafted and have taught a course on negotiation for about 15 years. In 1995, I received the school's prestigious award for teaching excellence in recognition of my venture into lecturing on a very complex and elusive subject.

Since there are no hard and fast rules in negotiation and the entire subject consists of utilizing various mental exercises and communication tactics, getting people to think intelligently about the stressful arena of negotiation is a formidable task. Nevertheless, it's a skill you will use your entire life—and Donald Trump's skill at negotiation is a large part of the reason he became a billionaire. My goal for this book is to help you think clearly about the complexities of negotiation, and more important, to make you a better negotiator.

1

WHAT IS
NEGOTIATION . . . REALLY?

I WANT TO START out by telling a story that will help you adopt the mind-set of an expert negotiator.

A multimillionaire had twin 10-year-old sons, one was an incurable optimist and the other an incurable pessimist. He thought to himself, "If I could get the optimist to be a little more pessimistic, and the pessimist a little more optimistic, I'd have two great boys." So on their birthday, the father arranged for each son's present to be delivered to the house. He bought the pessimist a $5,000 10-speed Japanese racing bike. Looking at the sleek red and silver model, he thought, "What could any 10-year-old possibly find wrong with this present? He should love it." For the optimist, he had two loads of horseshit dumped in the middle of his son's play room.

On the morning of their birthday, he visited the pessimist first and asked, "How do you like your present?"

"Like it?" said the boy, "I hate it. It's the worst thing you could have gotten me. If I take the bicycle outside I'll probably get hit by a bus and end up in the hospital with two broken legs. If I'm lucky and I do make it to the playground, some kid twice my size will beat the crap out of me and steal the bike. How could you be so thoughtless to give me a present like this?"

"Well, I really blew that one," thinks the father as he walks down the hall to check on his other son. He says to himself, "The other one is a sure winner." He opens the door to the playroom and sees the optimistic son sitting in the middle of the manure pile, throwing pieces all around the room. And he's singing!

"What *are* you doing?" the father asks.

The boy replies, "With all this shit, there's got to be a pony in here somewhere!"

That statement captures the mind-set of an experienced negotiator in a nutshell. You have to understand that a good negotiator learns how to go through a lot of shit to find the pony—a completed transaction. If you want to excel in negotiation, you must spend a lot of time exploring and learning what the other side really wants—in contrast to what they say they want. You have to ask a lot of questions to discover what they can live with and what they can't live with. You have to have a world of patience to continually probe for their strengths and weaknesses.

THE RULES OF NEGOTIATION

Before we go on, answer the following two questions:

1. *Are there any rules in negotiation?* The right answer is, "No, there are no rules in negotiation."
2. *Are lying, cheating, and deception permitted?* The right answer is "Yes, anything goes."

This doesn't mean that you should behave unethically or illegally. If Donald Trump makes a business deal, he keeps his word, and so will I. In fact I stress repeatedly in this book the need to build trust with the other side. However, a negotiation is not the same thing as a completed business transaction. Until the contract is signed, my experience is that everyone involved in the negotiation is free to act as he or she sees fit without restrictions.

For example, if the other side asks you, "Is this deal critical to you?" you can't candidly answer, "yes" or you'll be in a very weak position. You should say, "No, I'd like to complete this deal but I have others I can do if it doesn't work out."

I know of no sports or any competitive activity that grants such freedom to participants. For example, baseball, which is the favorite sport in the United States, has strict rules or guidelines. Each team can only field nine players at a time, a game consists of nine innings, an umpire determines which pitches are balls or strikes and has white lines that he uses to determine what is fair or foul. But negotiation, which is really "the game of life," has no rules or guidelines to determine how it is played and what constitutes fair or foul conduct. It is a series of communication exercises that inevitably lead to some conclusion. Only the parties involved can determine whether they won or lost or if there was a draw.

Negotiation Is Part of Life

Most people feel intimidated by the idea of negotiating, but the fact is, negotiation is something we've been doing all our lives, even when we don't realize it. I have been negotiating since I was born. The first time I was hungry I negotiated with my mother by screaming until she solved the problem by feeding me. I didn't do it consciously; it happened automatically.

You are in continual negotiation with everyone you meet, be it your boss or a casual friend. Boys negotiate with girls and vice versa. Husbands and wives constantly negotiate with each other. Negotiation makes its entrance when you buy a car or a house, or discuss with friends which movie to see. Negotiation isn't just concluding a difficult deal, it is daily participation in the game of life.

Many people think that the sole purpose in negotiating is getting the best deal you can. Donald Trump's approach, in contrast, is to pursue a course that enables the other parties to attain personal satisfaction as a by-product of his negotiation. Creating the atmosphere of an amicable relationship is more important than getting a deal done, than winning, or getting something the other person didn't want to give.

Trump earned his reputation as a great negotiator because of his insights into human nature. He understands how people think, how they can be motivated to embrace his ideas. He can craft the right strategy to help people to think outside of the box, looking *beyond* their self-imposed limitations rather than taking refuge behind them.

Although we have a tendency to believe that monetary rewards are far and away the prime motivator for people, it is more often the case that people are motivated by ego, prestige, recognition, or personal satisfaction. That's why Trump very rarely uses his money card in his negotiations. He has a dynamic, persuasive personality and he uses it expertly. Trump knows that the right words spoken at the right time can turn an adversary into a partner and convert a contentious disagreement into a mutually satisfactory working arrangement. For most people, that is where real negotiating skills comes into play to forge a result that is acceptable to everyone.

DEFINING NEGOTIATION

To be a good negotiator, you have to realize that negotiation is much more subtle than two people haggling about a price. Negotiation is our first form of communication with other people. *Negotiation is the sum of all the ways in which we convey information about what we want, what we desire, and what we expect from other people*—as well as how we receive information about other people's wants, desires, and expectations. Language is undoubtedly first in our arsenal of communication tools, but good negotiation involves much more than using appropriate language. It includes all the subtle and not-so-subtle ways we actually convey our desires.

We tend to think of negotiation as limited to talking, listening, and bargaining with someone else to achieve a desired result. Don't forget that negotiation has many other nonverbal forms. If someone is late for an appointment without an apology or doesn't show up at all, that is an element of negotiation as well. Sometimes what people don't do or say is the most telling factor—not taking a phone call, cutting a meeting short, or scheduling a conflicting meeting—these are all negotiation tactics of one kind or another. Anything that affects what you want from someone else, or what he or she wants from you (positively or negatively) is a negotiation.

Negotiation Always Means Compromise and Creativity

A basic fact of life is that we never get everything we want. So in the course I teach at New York University I tell my students that negotiation is *a process in which people learn to accept an available compromise as a satisfactory substitute for that which they thought they really wanted.*

Everybody goes into a transaction thinking that they know exactly what they want. But they usually can't get it, so they have to learn how to compromise along the way.

For example, if I go into a car dealership, I might start out by saying, "I'm looking for a sports car with four-wheel drive and a sun roof." Then I see a new model and say, "I really love that one. That's what I want."

The dealer tells me, "That has everything you said you wanted and it's only $36,000." I didn't intend to spend $36,000 for a car, so I tell the salesperson that's beyond my budget. The salesperson says, "I can show you two other models in the $25,000 range, but neither one has all the features you want. How important are those features to you?"

Eventually I have to forego some of the frills I wanted. . . . What I ended up with wasn't exactly what I originally had in mind but it was a satisfactory compromise for what I thought I *really* wanted. Every negotiation and everything you do in life has pluses or minuses—you have to weigh the pluses against the minuses—and a decision is reached when the pluses outweigh the minuses. It's that simple, although getting there often involves a lot of frustration, aggravation, and arguments.

What makes participation in a negotiation interesting is all the information you have to discover along the way, both about yourself and the other party. It's like trying to complete a jigsaw puzzle without a picture on the box to guide you and with an unknown quantity of pieces, and without shapes or colors to show where they go. Impossible? No. Difficult? Yes. Negotiation requires the use of brainpower and logic in lieu of any of the five senses. Commencing a negotiation can also be defined as starting a journey to an imaginary destination without a road map and where all the directions you're given are intentionally misleading. People will not be completely candid if they think it will jeopardize their desired result.

For example, Donald Trump rarely starts off any negotiation by telling the other side exactly what he really has in mind. As a case in point, let's analyze a specific, lengthy negotiation that took place between Donald Trump and Leonard Kandell relating to Donald's creation of Trump Tower, Trump's signature building on 5th Avenue in New York City. Kandell owned a building at East 57th Street that abutted both Tiffany & Co. and the parcel on which Trump Tower was to be built. Trump's control of the Kandell property was vital since it had valuable frontage on 57th Street and unused excess air rights that could be utilized to increase the height of Trump Tower. By carefully checking into Kandell's background, Trump learned that Kandell was a veteran developer and a hard-nosed, shrewd negotiator who favored long-term ownership of strategically located land over an outright sale. Donald really desired a long-term, flexible lease but knew that taking a direct approach would inevitably lead to protracted, difficult negotiations and a questionable result. Trump needed a wedge to get Kandell to consider granting him a long-term lease. While negotiating with Tiffany to buy its unused air rights, Trump learned that Tiffany had an option to buy the Kandell property at a price equal to its fair market value. As part of the air rights deal with Tiffany, Donald convinced Tiffany to transfer its option on the Kandell property to him.

Armed with the option, Trump then told Kandell that he was going to exercise the option and buy Kandell's property and asked Kandell how much he wanted for it. There were substantial disagreements and heated discussions between the parties as to what the fair market value was. It became apparent that arriving at fair market value and the transfer of title would probably require extensive and costly litigation. So Kandell invited Donald to lunch at the University Club in the hope of reaching a deal. Donald was certain that Kandell was going to offer him the long-term lease, which was what Donald really wanted, and he asked me to attend since I was familiar with the intricacies involved in a lease transaction. After some verbal sparring, as Trump had predicted, Kandell raised the possibility of a long-term ground lease. Trump said he needed an outright sale because he wanted to use the excess air rights. Kandell countered by saying if the rent was high enough he could make the air rights part of the ground lease. Trump asked, "Why would you want a long-term lease rather than several million dollars in cash?" In a moment of truth, Kandell replied that he didn't like the idea of paying the taxes resulting from the sale and he preferred leaving a long-term secure, cash-producing asset to his grandchildren rather than a lot of cash. Trump respected Kandell's honesty and immediately seized the opportunity to turn a potentially hostile negotiation into one of friendship and mutual trust. Trump said, "Len, that's not what I really had in mind, but if that's what you want and it will make you happy, I'll do it." They quickly agreed on the rental and other critical terms of the lease and shook hands on it. Before Donald left he said to me in front of Kandell, "Work out the details with Len. I want you to draw a lease that protects Len in every way but gives me what I really need to make Trump Tower a success." Trump's actions and demeanor between the handshake and his departure created an environment of trust that I was able to build on and use to avoid the unnecessary bickering that usually accompanies the drafting of important legal documents. Evidently, Trump's willingness to rely on me to finish the deal hit a responsive chord in Kandell. In an unusual move, he asked me, Donald's attorney, to prepare the lease. Recognizing this display of confidence, I told him I would protect his interests as if he were my client. Within two weeks the lease was prepared, negotiated, and signed. Both Trump and Kandell ultimately got what they really wanted in the deal but we all got much more.

As a direct result of the amicable conclusion of the negotiation, Trump and Kandell established a friendship that lasted until Kandell died. Kandell later asked me to be his lawyer because of the feeling of trust that had been created. A similar relationship exists between his heirs and me. The moral of this story is, "Sometimes directly asking for what you want is not the best way to achieve a desired result."

As this story shows, good negotiation is a *continual exploration of the realm of possibilities*. In many cases, your success is going to depend on your ability to think in reverse, something Trump is a master of. Thinking in reverse comes into play when you make a proposal that is so outrageous that you know it has no chance of acceptance in its raw form and then reversing your course and agreeing to modify your proposal to make it more palatable for the other side. In the process of coming up with mutually acceptable solutions, you have to consider multiple options. The more bait you throw in the water, the more likely you will catch a fish.

As another example, I might start out thinking I need a basic laptop computer. But the salesperson might say, "Here's a basic unit that's only $599 but it's not what you need." Why not? Is he helping me make a better decision, or enticing me to spend more money or to buy the model with the greatest profit margin? The computer salesperson, like every other negotiator, is always selling something. This is where I begin my journey toward that imaginary destination. What about one with a 50 megabyte capacity with a 4× CD-ROM internal drive? I know I need a computer, but the details are fuzzy since I actually don't know a megabyte from a mosquito bite. I need to negotiate my way into getting reliable information, but without being seduced by the salesperson's gift of gab. Maybe only a higher priced model will serve my needs. An in-depth discussion is needed before I make a purchase. Creativity, skepticism, information gathering, and willingness to consider multiple solutions are all key elements you must master if you want to be a good negotiator.

What Negotiation Is *Not*

There are three things that you need to know in understanding negotiation. First, it is not a science. Second, it is not a situation in which winning is everything. Third, it is not an event with continuity—the parties involved, their motives, and their goals are all different and are all subject to change at any moment during the course of the negotiation.

It Is Not a Science: The Key Role of Satisfaction

One aspect that absolutely everyone wants from a negotiation is a feeling of satisfaction with the final outcome. To succeed in a negotiation, you have to persuade and lead the other side into sharing a state of satisfaction—you can't force that feeling on them. However, satisfaction is a purely subjective emotional state that is directly linked to a person's personality. You very rarely achieve something in negotiation that is entirely tangible, or can be proven or even effectively measured. Science, on the other hand, is precise. You know what you have achieved, and it can be quantified in tangible form. A negotiation cannot meet that criteria. So if someone asks you, "Did you win or lose in that negotiation?" you are not going to be able to give a definitive answer. You probably won some points and lost others, but the concept of winning or losing is just too precise and limited to explain how real life negotiations end up. There are no absolute right or wrong answers in a negotiation.

Sometimes a phase of negotiation ends up with an entirely different outcome than you expected or desired. And yet, you discovered that satisfaction and peace of mind were more important than the price you paid. The feeling of comfort may be more meaningful to you than getting the best price. Satisfaction should be your real goal, not the best price or getting everything you asked for. It is a human process with limitless nuances and complexities, and not fulfilled by merely reaching agreement on cost and performance.

It Is Not a Situation in Which Winning Is Everything

There is invariably so much more involved than the simple concept of winning or losing. That is a binary approach based on the idea that you go into a negotiation with something very specific in mind, and you come out getting that exact outcome, or losing altogether. This point of view—there must be a winner and a loser—is shortsighted and doomed to fail. In a truly successful negotiation, you have to establish *trust* and a *friendly relationship* as part of the process and a crucial element of the outcome. If you trust a plumber to stick to his estimate and fix a problem, you will be happy to use him over and over and willingly pay his specified price. If you don't feel a sense of trust, you would be smart to look elsewhere. The same holds true for a car dealer, financial planner, or real estate expert or any other party with whom you are contemplating a relationship.

It Is Not an Event with Continuity

Most negotiations consist of a series of several separate negotiations of assorted sizes and shapes. There is rarely a single discussion or meeting that has a clear beginning and end. So what usually occurs, over the course of any negotiation is a change of circumstances, or additional factors arise that cause people to change their positions. You can't always assume that something said yesterday will still be true today.

For example, let's assume that you have a car to sell, and that I want to buy it. I think we have a deal, so I will talk to you tomorrow. But meanwhile, the circumstances change. You get a phone call from someone with a better offer. Someone else needs the car and because we broke off the discussion for a day, the continuity was lost. The phone call you received was a new factor that colored our negotiation, so your position is different. This happens all the time in ongoing negotiations, and you can use it to your advantage as you will see in later chapters when I talk about slowing down or speeding up a negotiation.

SEVEN GOALS TO HELP YOU SUCCEED IN ANY NEGOTIATION

Although you can't be sure where you'll end up, it's still important to set goals when you begin any negotiation. I'm going to give you seven goals to help you become more effective as a negotiator:

Goal 1: I want to profit from the negotiation. However, the definition of *profit* in this context is not necessarily financial. Profiting from a negotiation often involves discovering some benefit you had not even considered at the outset. Going in with an open mind is extremely useful. You are likely to learn much more from being prepared to anticipate the possibility of an unexpected outcome, than you are if you are only narrowly focused on a single, predetermined idea.

Goal 2: I want to learn as much as I can about the people on the other side. Everyone has a story that relates to why and how he or she is entering into a negotiation, and it is rarely what you would assume. If you are able to find the other person's story—if you ask questions—you will inevitably find out something valuable that can help you in later negotiations. Adopting an approach that meets the needs of other parties will help you build trust and build a relationship, which are key elements of any negotiation. For example, in my office I have some dollar bills in a frame on the wall. People ask me why I have them up there. It gives me a chance to tell them those were the dollars I won when people bet me that I couldn't do something. That's part of *my* story, and it tells you something about my character and how I might be expected to behave in a negotiation.

Goal 3: I want to find out where the bottom line is. What is the minimum the other side says it has to have, or there's no deal, and what is the maximum you will give, or you'll walk away? Everything between those two extremes is negotiable—I call it the *zone of uncertainty*. It is essential to discover the other side's bottom line and to establish the zone of uncertainty, if you want to negotiate effectively. While you're attempting to quantify the zone of uncertainly, you should assume the other side is trying to do the same thing.

Remember, people are not going to be truthful when it comes to telling you what their bottom line is. Many don't really know what it is, and those who claim to know are not always right. So defining the other party's bottom line is something you develop through discussion and observation, and not only by what they tell you it is.

Goal 4: I want to understand the constraints surrounding the transaction. Some people have to finish a transaction within a specific time frame, for example, year end. Maybe he doesn't have the necessary authority to conclude a deal but requires approval from someone else. These constraints are going to dictate how someone negotiates with you.

Goal 5: I want to study the other side. To negotiate effectively, you have to obtain the essential information you need to know. You can do this through direct discussions and by talking to other parties. You need to learn as much as you can about the personalities involved, their knowledge of the subject matter, their education levels, and their negotiating abilities. Assembling all of this information (to the extent possible) will reveal the best way to deal with another person. If someone is prone to using crude language or telling off-color jokes, you will connect better with him by responding in kind. If someone is very serious, all business, humorless, he will probably feel most comfortable if you adopt a similar style. You need to find out whether the other person is reputed to be honorable or has a reputation for playing dirty. Will the other person keep his word, or will he try to weasel out of prior statements? This is crucial information you need in order to know how to effectively act, respond, and communicate with the other side.

Goal 6: I want to assess the people on my side in any negotiation. By "my side," I mean anyone who will help me participate in this transaction. That includes anyone that you report to, the money people, lawyers, or if the negotiation is of a personal nature, your spouse, or parents, for example. Anyone who has ever thought about buying a house knows what I mean by this. Your spouse might fall for a particular feature of the house, while you think it's overpriced. So how will you deal with this difference of opinion? You need to find a way to bridge the gap to reach an acceptable compromise. When you present your position to the other side, you need to understand the difference between posture and reality. The posture—the face you put forward in the negotiation—is not necessarily an accurate reflection of reality. For example, you and your spouse might disagree about whether to make an offer for a house. Your spouse might want to proceed, but you think the price is too high. So you might go to the realtor and say, "The kitchen needs extensive renovation. That's why my offer might be lower than you wanted."

That's an example of posturing. You shouldn't tell the realtor, "My wife loves the house and thinks we should offer the asking price, but I think it is overpriced." While it is true, it indicates dissention in the ranks and weakens your negotiating position.

Goal 7: I need to find out what is fair and reasonable. In every phase of every negotiation, everyone says, "I only want what is fair and reasonable." Unfortunately, each side has a different opinion of what "fair and reasonable" is when applied to solve a particular issue. Extensive probing is necessary to find out what others deem fair and reasonable and how it differs from your opinion.

CONCLUSION

I've always maintained that the best negotiators in the world are two-year-olds. If they don't get what they want right away, they lie on the floor and scream and hold their breath until they do get what they want. They won't shut up until they win. The parent may beg, plead, and give the child anything he or she wants to get them to stop; so the child wins that negotiation—and learns that the tantrums work. Or the parent is strong enough to ignore the bad behavior and walks away leaving the infant screaming, kicking, and so on. The parent has decided to use a different negotiating tactic. From that, the child eventually learns that the tantrums don't achieve the desired result, so the tactic will be abandoned in favor of one that does work, such as throwing his arms around a parent and saying: "I love you, Mom." In either case, both sides learn something from the negotiation, which will help them in future negotiations. If you pay attention, you will learn something from every negotiation you're involved in that can improve your skills as a negotiator. My hope is that this book conveys to you some of the things Donald Trump and I have learned from our many years of deal making and thousands of high-level business negotiations. In the next chapter, I am going to begin by telling you how to negotiate like Donald Trump. In a series of step-by-step chapters, I'll go through the phases and strategies that will help you understand the art of negotiation.

Why should you bother to study the art of negotiation? Why should you read this book? Because an experienced and sophisticated negotiator is always going to get better results in any life situation than someone who is not knowledgeable about these techniques. In many cases, this is the difference between total success and dismal failure.

Let's get started. . . .

2

HONE YOUR PERSONALITY

Build Trust, Friendship,
and Satisfaction with
the Other Side

S OME PEOPLE THINK negotiation is a matter of listing your demands, somehow persuading the other side to agree with you, writing or receiving a check, and going home early. No. If that ever happens to you, you've made a bad deal. Quality negotiation takes a major expenditure of time. Negotiation requires that you reach out to the other side, sympathize, and create *real* interest that flows in both directions. A good negotiation should never be accomplished by a one-way communication.

Often, your financial status, and other seemingly important factors don't matter as much as your ability to make favorable connections with the people with clout. Trump has always had that ability. For example, when Donald Trump decided to open a casino in Atlantic City, it was a whole new venture and he had no prior experience. Why did Trump think he could successfully run a casino? How could he meet the standards imposed by the regulators (New Jersey Division of Gaming Enforcement)? At first glance, opening a casino didn't make sense for Donald Trump. But understand one guiding principle in business: It's not the nature of a particular transaction that really matters, but your background, reputation, and track record.

Ironically, Trump's lack of casino experience was a plus in this case. Because of gambling's shady history, the regulators didn't want people with experience. They look for someone with a track record of running profitable businesses, who has the ability to raise the money a casino requires, and who knows how to run a successful operation. During the casino approval process, Trump had to answer many tough questions, but his impeccable background, excellent reputation, and track record of accomplishments carried him through successfully. In addition, Trump always fosters political contacts, and he had influential people willing to vouch for him. This helped influence the decision makers.

If you are entering a negotiation, you will be much stronger if you can convince the other side of your qualifications in advance. Your first priority is to convince the decision makers that you can do what you propose. Furnish the proof you need to back up your statements. In this example, Trump made a great opening statement of his qualifications to the members of the New Jersey Casino Control Commission. It explained he would show them that it was in *their* best interests to give him the green light. Whatever additional information they required was prepared carefully and furnished in a timely manner to enforce Trump's reputation of trustworthiness. When you can demonstrate that you mean what you say, you will be believed from that time on.

THE GOALS OF ANY NEGOTIATION: TRUST, RAPPORT, AND SATISFACTION

Next I describe eight tips for conducting what I consider to be an intelligent negotiation. Sure, you can play dirty, intimidate the other side, and sometimes even get a better deal than you thought possible. You can also get rich robbing banks if you don't get caught. But would you want to live that way, taking things from other people and building a reputation that is so bad that nobody wants to deal with you? You will lose much more by being underhanded than you can possibly gain. I have earned my reputation as a tough but fair negotiator who is a deal maker and whose word can be trusted.

I believe that success in any negotiation comes down to the creation of three things: trust, rapport, and satisfaction.

Trust is the cement of all good-faith dealings between people. Don't even consider dealing with someone you can't trust—you can never protect yourself from a thief. The best you can hope for is aggravation and costly litigation. Life is too short to go looking for trouble no matter how good the deal looks. An environment of mutual trust works for both sides. It removes doubt and suspicion from the transaction. It ensures that the discussions can go forward without that nagging fear that the other side is taking undue advantage of a situation.

Trust does not mean simply agreeing to the other side's demands. Except for immoral or illegal tactics, you can use any course of conduct you desire to gain the upper hand in a negotiation. Trump style negotiation is a tough game; he plays hard and plays to win. I recommend you use any available psychological technique that enables you to gain and keep an advantage. Feel free to make statements that you know are only posturing rather than real bottom-line positions. But everything can be accomplished within the framework of trust—not in what you say, but what you have finally agreed to do. It is my honest opinion, based on 50 years' experience, that without learning how to create an atmosphere of trust, you will never become a truly successful negotiator.

The next attribute, *rapport*, might seem irrelevant at first. I have included it because my experience has proven time and again that I cannot successfully negotiate with someone unless a level of affinity exists between us. This doesn't mean I have to invite the person over for a weekend barbecue or to go sailing but that's not a bad idea if I think it will help. Because of his billionaire status, Donald Trump has an unlimited array of things he can offer to convince the other side that he'll be great to work with. With a specially designed, luxurious 727 at his disposal, he can whisk people he wants to impress to his five-star private club in Palm Beach for a weekend when Elton John is entertaining. Or his private helicopter can fly them to Atlantic City where they may stay in the Alexander Suite, a 4,000-square-foot penthouse at the top of his Taj Mahal Hotel. Maybe a round of golf at one of his four world-class golf clubs will help break the ice.

I am certain that few of my readers can come anywhere close to those perks. But you can do something different that can also work. One day Donald Trump and I were walking through one of his buildings in which a new marble floor was being installed in the lobby by a workman. As we passed, Donald said to me in a loud voice, "George, you see this guy? He's the best marble man in the city." He patted the laborer on the shoulder and said, "Keep up the good work." Was Trump negotiating with this worker? Of course he was. From that moment on you can be sure that the man's work product would be of the best quality because of the compliment Trump bestowed on him. There's a valuable lesson to be learned from this incident. Treat everyone you meet with respect, no matter what his or her station in life and you will reap rewards that will cost you nothing.

Here's another example of a creative way someone built trust and rapport with me in the context of a negotiation. One of my responsibilities at the Trump Organization involved the successful launch of Trump Ice—bottled, high-quality natural spring water. Part of my job was to pick exclusive distributors in various areas of the United States and let them sell Trump Ice. A potential distributor of Trump Ice in Minneapolis, who really wanted the product, learned that I would be at a book signing in the Mall of America on a given date. He asked if I could give him an hour there to do something unusual that he thought I would like. I said okay and he asked, "What's your favorite number?" I said, "Sixteen because that's my anniversary date and I've been happily married for over fifty years." When I arrived in Minneapolis he picked me up at the airport, drove me to my hotel, and it was then I learned that he had arranged for me to go to the Minnesota Twins stadium where I could throw out the first ball and he gave me a Twins uniform to change into with "Ross" and "16" on the back. He drove me to the Twins stadium where a police escort took me directly onto the playing field. Someone handed me a baseball and the man on the PA system announced that I would throw the first pitch. There I was, a 76-year-old lawyer for Donald Trump, in a Twins uniform, throwing a ceremonial pitch in front of a packed stadium of cheering baseball fans. Oh yeah, I managed to reach the catcher at home plate and the umpire gave me a gratuitous strike call. On the way out I thought, if this guy is so creative and motivated, I should give him the Minnesota distributorship rights for Trump Ice. We negotiated the deal before I left Minneapolis and it's been a great deal for both of us.

Of course my celebrity status as one of the stars of *The Apprentice* helped him get the cooperation he needed to pull off this event, but it was his idea of an inexpensive, creative way to foster a feeling of rapport. As a natural offshoot of trust, some form of rapport is a necessary ingredient for success. It simply makes the whole discussion move along better. It helps turn an adversary into an ally who feels like a friend. With that hurdle behind me, I can appeal to the other side to work *with* me to create a deal that meets the needs of everyone in my organization and their organization. You may be able to do that without creating a feeling of rapport but it's much more tedious and difficult.

Rapport implies something beyond trust. Just as it is impossible make a good deal with someone you cannot trust, it is equally impossible to get to a mutually satisfying result if the two sides are not "tuned in" to one another. "Rapport" in the context of a business deal implies mutual respect, a genuine sense of liking each other, and a willingness to modify a deal as you move through the process—as long as both sides can reach a mutually acceptable solution to each issue.

This brings me to the third attribute, *satisfaction*. I think there is a great misconception out there in the world that you should enter a negotiation with a single, ruthless goal in mind: to win. If that's what you think, you couldn't be farther off base. The goal should be for both sides to get something they can live with and leave with a feeling of satisfaction, and a willingness to do another deal at a later time. If you end a negotiation with the other side feeling betrayed, abused, or unfairly taken advantage of, all you've really accomplished is the creation of an enemy who may come back to haunt you.

I once negotiated with someone who unnecessarily turned me into an enemy. I was representing a major developer who had procured a large loan from a major life insurance company. As part of the loan, my client was obligated to pay the legal fees of the lender's attorneys. But when the bill came, even though I myself was a high-priced lawyer I thought these charges were outrageous. When I called to complain that the fees were excessive, the partner of the lender's law firm told me, "There's nothing to discuss, that's what your client must pay if you want to close the loan." My client paid the fee but in my subsequent deals I insisted that that same lender avoid using that law firm if it wanted to make the loan. By taking such a firm and unreasonable stand, that law firm made me an enemy for life and it missed out on other transactions where it could have made millions of dollars in fees.

Some people think that it would be totally satisfying to win completely and to have the other side lose completely. But that only engenders the thought that you could have asked for more and gotten it. So you're not really satisfied with the result. By definition, negotiation is compromise, give-and-take, and the creation of a mutually acceptable deal. If a negotiator simply seeks to crush the opposition, he isn't a negotiator; he's just a bully who achieved his desired result by using a position of power. Ultimately, he shoots himself in the foot because that reputation follows him around forever.

People are more likely to negotiate with you when you have the reputation of being fair, no matter how great an advantage you may have. That reputation comes from leaving the other party with a sense of satisfaction that they got the most they could under the circumstances.

These three attributes, *trust, rapport, and satisfaction*, are so important to me that I always have them in mind as initial *goals* when I enter into a negotiation. Sure, there are points I have to win and other points I'd like to win; but to make the negotiation a successful one, it has to be based on these three attributes, or it just isn't worth the effort.

EIGHT TIPS FOR BUILDING TRUST, RAPPORT, AND SATISFACTION

Trust, rapport, and satisfaction are the big-picture goals in Trump-style negotiation, but how do you achieve them? Here are the ways:

1. Find common ground with the other side.
2. Establish a good rapport.
3. Be a nice person to deal with.
4. Find the appropriate level of communication.
5. Understand the other side and its needs.
6. Cement feelings of trust.
7. Learn flexibility.
8. Become known as a deal maker and not as a deal breaker.

The best starting point—always—is to *find common ground with the other side*. It doesn't matter how small the common ground is or what its nature is; you need to find it and use that as the base for going forward. This is much more than just discovering you both like golf or fishing, or have children the same age, or agree on politics or laugh at the same jokes. It's the limitless range of interesting things you can find out about people just by talking with them. If you rush into the dollars and cents discussion of a negotiation without laying this groundwork first, you will have an unpleasant experience, and more likely than not, an unsatisfactory outcome.

When I ask a question or start a conversation with the other side, it might seem like banter and small talk. But I'm searching for the basis of a connection. Without being obvious, I'm figuring out how to get into the other person's persona. If you compliment people on pictures of their kids, you might discover that those kids are at the center of the person's life. Or you might find out the kids are a pain and bring their parents a lot of grief. This is information that may later be helpful on many levels, because it increases your knowledge of what makes the other side tick.

Trump's office is a good example. What do you see when you look around? He has dozens of pictures of himself on magazine covers, with Bill Clinton, Shaquille O'Neil, and numerous starlets and glamorous women. There are many sports figures, which tells you Donald is a big sports fan. You can also tell right away that he likes beautiful women. If you had never heard of Donald Trump before visiting his office, you would be able to pick up a lot of information about him just from looking around. You would guess that he would rather talk about sports than classical music—not as a certainty, but as a pretty good guess. Armed with information and insight about the person, you are more likely to be able to convince that person of something very important. One excellent way to find a common ground is to speak to people who have done business or are friendly with the other side. Often you can find useful information by searching the Internet. Explore any avenue that may get you background information.

Second, you *establish a good rapport* by talking and listening, remembering always the reasons for this step. I've found that once I have good rapport with someone, I get more straightforward answers from him or her. This beginning of feeling comfortable grows out of your own sincerity, an expression of your genuine interest in the other person. It doesn't relate specifically to what you're negotiating about. But if you want it to go well, you need to begin with good rapport. Now, not only are you a good negotiator who understands the other person, but you can sell yourself, convince the person that you can do a better job than anyone else, that the transaction will be problem free, that your word can be depended on, and that "everything is going to be okay."

Third, you should *be a nice person to deal with.* This is a no-brainer from my point of view. Working with a nice person is the most pleasant course for anyone to take, and you want to make it as easy as possible for the other side to feel content doing business with you. It involves far more work and effort to be aggressive, argumentative, and offensive—not to mention that it's exhausting. The primary thing to remember, though, is that nice people are better negotiators and they get a higher percentage of satisfying outcomes.

Fourth, *find the appropriate level and style of communication* with the other side. It doesn't make sense to have just one approach or negotiating style and to use it everywhere. Today I might be negotiating with an extroverted person who wants to talk in the bar while telling off-color jokes and enjoying a good New York martini. Tomorrow I might meet with someone who is all-business, has no sense of humor, and doesn't drink. Clearly, I would face a potential disaster if I applied today's experience to the person I meet tomorrow. You shouldn't come across as fake, but your style of communication has to work for the specific circumstances and for the specific person.

Fifth, *understand the other side and its needs.* I'll go into this in detail in a later chapter. For now, though, just remember that part of that creation of trust, friendship, and satisfaction has to come from your understanding what makes the other side tick. Some people need acknowledgment or respect, and others need to feel that they are in control. One of your first objectives in any negotiation should be to find out what they *need* in the negotiation. And more to the point, how do you deal with those needs?

For example, let's say I figure out early on that the other side must feel they are "winning" the negotiation. A smart way for me to get them to trust me, develop rapport, and gain a sense of satisfaction, is for me to make lots of small concessions. Let them win everything that's unimportant but nothing that is critical to your position. In every negotiation, you have a list of points you want to win; some are major and others are minor. Surrender the minor ones reluctantly but only after you have made a credible attempt at trying to win them. Use all your negotiating strategies to keep from surrendering the major ones. Using this approach, you achieve two advantages. First, you satisfy their natural human desire to think they are winning. Second, you accumulate negotiating points for later on, when you start dealing with the other issues on the list. Having made small concessions early on, you're more likely to win the bigger points that really matter.

Sixth, *cement feelings of trust* during your negotiation. Establishing trust initially is fairly easy because it requires sincerity and a friendly approach to the other side. But once you start talking about the details of the deal, you need to constantly reinforce those feelings so they're not lost or diminished. You establish your own reputation for trustworthiness by meticulously keeping your promises, remaining sincere and friendly, and always—always—keeping in mind what the other side needs to be satisfied. All of this cements the essential element of trust that you were smart enough to create.

There are two things every negotiator should know about trust. First, there is always going to be a severe "discount factor" when there is a lack of trust. You never know what that discount factor amounts to because it's not finite. It affects the outcome but cannot be measured. If the other side doesn't trust you, they're going to charge you a higher price, or they're not going to be willing to make concessions or, for that matter, to make even a small leap of faith. If during any negotiation, someone says to you, "Trust me on this" a warning siren should go off in your brain. If he is trustworthy, his actions will display that fact. If he tells you, he's probably trying to get you to lower your guard so that he can successfully utilize some devious strategy.

29

Once the "no-trust discount" is in place, then all credibility is shot. The negotiation cannot proceed in a straightforward manner and the discount colors every discussion. The second thing to remember about trust is that people are always willing to pay a premium for peace of mind. If you can gain the other side's trust, you have a clear advantage over any competitor who is saddled with the discount factor because they aren't trusted.

NO ONE EVER ASKS FOR A POUND OF FRIENDSHIP OR A BUCKET OF INTEGRITY BUT THEY *WILL* PAY YOU FOR IT IF YOU DELIVER IT

Always keep the discount and premium principles in mind throughout every negotiation. The other side will pay a premium for peace of mind and confidence in your integrity. This "raises your stock" and removes one of the most prevalent obstacles that is often found in most negotiations—whether you're dealing with a real estate owner, a spouse, or a car salesman. It applies to everything.

Seventh, *learn flexibility* in your negotiations. I have observed time and again that inflexible negotiations are usually doomed to fail. You need to be able to "go with the flow," and to adjust your style to the people involved, the issues, and the sticking points you discover along the way. Remember the saying, "If your only tool is a hammer, you see every problem as a nail." Hitting every problem one way just doesn't work. Some problems have to be modified, refined, or reshaped before they can be solved.

So if I am in a negotiation with someone and it's a real estate deal, how do I operate using the Trump style? Am I going to go in there and try to pressure the other side to accept an ultimatum? I could say, "We always close our deals in 60 days, take it or leave it." But that would be a mistake. I would rather start out saying, "You know, I like to think that this deal can be closed in 60 days if both sides are willing to work at it." The other party might come back at me and say, "I need at least 90 days."

Here's where flexibility can be a very useful tool. I don't know if the other side is posturing or making a must-be statement. I can ask, "Why is that?" The answer could give me valuable insight into the mind-set of the opposition. The truth is, I don't need to close in 60 days, but the other side doesn't know that. When and if I give that up, I want something in return. So a big part of what I call "flexibility" also involves being smart about the timing and content of my statements and positions. Like every good poker player, keep your cards to your vest and don't show the other players more than you have to.

Eighth and last, you should strive to *become known as a deal maker and not as a deal breaker*. Deal breakers never win negotiations they just end them. If you get the reputation of being a deal breaker, the best and most interesting deals will never come your way. Those go to the deal makers. Many people walk away from perfectly good deals because their ego won't let them make the final small concessions needed to successfully conclude a negotiation. In case you doubt the role that "ego" plays in negotiation, here's a true story to illustrate it. My wife and I were on vacation in Acapulco. While we were lying on the beach, we noticed a peddler selling Mexican blankets to the tourists. When he opened a very colorful one my wife said to me, "I really love that one. I wonder how much it is?" "I'll find out," I replied and left the cool shade of my umbrella to check it out. The temperature of the sand on the beach must have been 200 degrees and I am sure the sight of an American tourist hopping toward him warmed the vendor's heart. He must have thought, "Here's a live fish." I asked him the price of the blanket. "$40 American," he said. I replied, "Is your name Pancho Villa?" (the notorious Mexican bandit) "because that price is much too high!" He laughed and replied, "How much would you pay for it?" I countered with, "$10 American." He scoffed at my offer and said, "That wouldn't even pay for the wool." I said, "What wool? It looks like rope to me." With that he folded the blanket and picked up his wares and walked away and I went back to my cozy umbrella.

My wife asked, "How much was it?" I said, "I don't know yet. We are negotiating the price." After an hour passed, the blanket salesman came back and again held up the blanket in question. He signaled with his fingers, "$35." I signaled back, "$11." For three more hours the negotiations continued until finally he said he would sell it for $15.50. But I had already dug in my heels with an offer of $15.00. Now here's where the "ego" took over and killed the deal. As a matter of pride, neither of us would budge. As a result, the sale was never made—because of 50 cents! My inexperience in negotiation let my ego affect my decision and the ego of the vendor killed the deal. Warning: In your negotiations, don't let your ego control your brain and force you to do things that are not in your best interest. Sometimes you have to swallow your pride to be a successful negotiator.

As I said before, success in negotiating does not mean winning; it does mean being creative enough to bypass or overcome the stumbling blocks, to defuse all contentious confrontations, and working with the other side to arrive at mutually acceptable solutions that may bear little or no resemblance to the initial problem. A deal maker should be willing to give up some of the points he originally said were "must haves" while keeping the ones that are essential to the viability of the deal. Deal makers are people who can convince the other side that they can work with them to solve the issues that inevitably crop up and will find a way to make the deal happen.

Be a Chameleon—Adapt Your Negotiating Style to the Negotiating Environment

The importance of the eight tips and three goals does not mean you should be the same or act the same way in every negotiation. Remember the saying, "Different strokes for different folks." Learn to be a chameleon. Change your appearance to successfully blend in with the negotiating environment. If the other side is screaming—scream back. If the discussions are quiet and controlled—be quiet and controlled. A chameleon's greatest weapon is its ability to change at will. You also have to learn to change your negotiating style immediately if something you're doing isn't working. Raising your voice when others are quiet or speaking quietly when others are shouting may also get you the attention you desire.

This isn't the same as being flexible. When I say you should be flexible, I mean you look for mutually acceptable creative solutions. Being a chameleon is a matter of displaying a particular negotiating style at a particular time. A chameleon always blends in with its surroundings. A good negotiator has the ability to blend in harmonious fashion with the tone, mood, and people in the room when it's in his best interest to do so but can quickly change tactics when necessary to achieve a desired effect.

For example, Donald Trump has impressive personal skills and he knows how to quickly assess the other side, to seize and recognize the mood, and to go with it when it suits his purposes. I'm a chameleon in the sense that I'm always ready to take punches when necessary but can quickly adjust my personal style to steer the negotiation to the path that will lead to the conclusion I desire. Believe me when I say that mastery of this trait is essential to every good negotiator.

How do you know which personal style or tone to adopt? Seemingly, trivial information you gain about the other side along the way may give you an insight into the best strategy. For example, you might see a much-cluttered desk that leads you to suspect the guy is either disorganized or overwhelmed. It might be a useful and effective tactic to assure him that you will take care of the details, get the forms, fill them out, and take the administrative burdens off his back. But if you start down that path and he disagrees, you should change your tactics immediately. Remember you're a chameleon. So you might say, "Well, I'm happy that you will see that all the details are properly taken care of since it'll make my job much easier."

In the next chapter, I help you take the next step to becoming a crackerjack negotiator. Once you have established trust and rapport (although often this happens simultaneously), the next step in a negotiation is to begin searching out the other side's wish list and identifying their strengths and weaknesses. In the process, you will almost always uncover useful and important information that will give you an advantage in the negotiation.

3

PROBE TO LEARN WHAT
THE OTHER SIDE
WANTS, FLUSH OUT
WEAKNESSES, AND UNCOVER
IMPORTANT INFORMATION

WHEN I NEGOTIATE, I start out trying to discover what motivates the person across the table. He or she might be an optimist who feels certain that there will be a successful outcome, or a pessimist who is convinced that I will pull a fast one on them and they'll end up with a lousy deal. If so, I have to win the pessimist over and get to know him or her better before I have the right to expect our negotiation to end well.

A joke like the pony joke at the beginning of Chapter 1 is a good ice breaker because it sets a relaxed tone while establishing the point that negotiation requires patience. Using some inoffensive humor (like the pony joke) is often a good way to start out a negotiation—building the relationship with the other side and getting the discussion going on a more personal, human level. By using an old style of negotiation, where personalities don't count, both parties entrench themselves in specific positions and slug it out to get as much from the other side as possible, is not nearly as rewarding or as successful as Trump-style negotiation that always strives to leave the door open for future negotiation if the need arises.

A FUNDAMENTAL RULE: DON'T ACCEPT ANYTHING AT FACE VALUE

As a smart negotiator, you should verify *everything*. You have to make various assumptions and work with the facts you're given throughout all phases of any negotiation but until they are tested for accuracy, don't trust them. You must continuously test each of your assumptions to find the extent to which it is right or wrong. This is a fundamental rule of Trump-style negotiating. Some information that you will be given will not be what it seems; it will be partially true and partially false. The key is to start out with the belief that all of your assumptions and estimates about the other side are wrong and then be pleasantly surprised to learn some of them were right.

Does this mean you don't trust people or believe what they say? Of course not! You *build* trust and assess truthfulness through the process of discussion and negotiation, but never start out taking the other side at face value. For example, if I'm going into a real estate negotiation, my initial assumption might be that the other side wants to sell a particular building at the price they have in mind and that I'm the right buyer. But I need to test out even this very basic assumption.

The following questions would be appropriate to ask: How long have you owned the property? Why do you want to sell it now? What makes you think it's worth what you're asking? Who are the real owners of the property? How many mortgages are there on the property and who holds them? The answers and how they are given will definitely influence my negotiation strategy.

Here's an example of how to test assumptions and analyze "facts" presented to you by the other side in a negotiation. Let's say a property is listed for sale at $3 million *firm*. Since the price is listed as a "firm price," most people assume that's the price that must be paid to buy the property—period. But my experience tells me that the listed price is often just a way for the seller to test the market. When I was a real estate consultant at Edward S. Gordon Company, a broker who worked there told me he had seen an apartment he loved and it was listed at a price of $3 million "firm." He asked me how much he should offer for it. I asked him, "How much are you thinking of offering?" He answered, "I want to offer $2.6 million and settle for $2.8 million. What do you think?" He was shocked when I said, "I would offer $1.2 million."

"That's crazy!" he said, "They'll be insulted because that offer is much too low!"

I explained, "The worst that can happen is that they'll turn you down cold and not even discuss it further. But maybe they'll start negotiating to try to reach a mutually acceptable price. Try it and see what happens." He followed my advice and ended up buying the apartment for $2.4 million—$400,000 less than he was willing to pay, and $600,000 below the "firm" price of $3 million!

IMPORTANT FACT TO REMEMBER: DON'T BELIEVE EVERYTHING SOMEONE WRITES OR SAYS

There's a great line from Gilbert and Sullivan's *H.M.S. Pinafore*. "Things are seldom what they seem/Skim milk masquerades as cream." Any assumption you make based on something you've heard, seen, deduced, or been told could be completely wrong.

I recall many years ago starting out a negotiation with a well-known real estate mogul here in New York. When I was ushered into his massive office, he was lying on a couch wearing an old straw hat. He didn't even stand up and greet me. The first thing he said was, "Trust me, I will always make a fair deal." As soon as he made that statement, I knew he was lying. A person shouldn't have to tell me he can be trusted to act fairly, he should convince me by his conduct throughout the negotiation. This was skim milk masquerading as cream.

FEARS AND WISHES INFLUENCE PERCEPTION ON BOTH SIDES

If someone is worried that things will go wrong in a deal, he or she will be a timid and hesitant negotiator. His or her fear will manifest itself throughout the negotiation, make him or her weak and overly eager to make a deal. It puts him or her at a disadvantage. The attitudes and preconceived ideas of any party will taint the entire negotiation.

For example, let's assume you go into a negotiation fearful that you won't be able to complete the deal in time. Your boss has given you a one-week deadline, so you're already at a disadvantage. You're working under severe pressure. If nothing happens within a week, you have to explain it to your boss who will probably be unhappy with your performance. That forced deadline inhibits your negotiating ability. One solution is to ask your boss, "Why is one week so critical?" If he sticks to the deadline, tell him you'll do your best but you probably won't get the most favorable deal that might be available. Perhaps you can convince him that there is more to be gained by going slow and negotiating cautiously. Be aware that fears and wishes influence everyone's actions, but look for ways to minimize them.

IT'S WRONG TO ASSUME THAT THE OTHER SIDE KNOWS WHAT YOU KNOW

Now let's take a look at the other side's assumptions. During the course of the negotiation, I verify my assumptions about the other side and I assume they're checking me out as well. What do they know about my negotiating objectives?

The other side might not know anything at all, but they are going to operate on their own series of assumptions. So perhaps it's absolutely essential for me to contract to sell a property by the end of the month. I don't want them to know that because that could severely hamper my negotiating power. If I wrongfully assume they already know my plight, I will negotiate accordingly. Let them ferret out what factors will govern my negotiating strategy. Don't be helpful and volunteer any information that could be used against you. Even in a difficult situation like that, you can offer a great deal of information that doesn't actually re-veal the weaknesses in your position. You can be friendly and, at the same time, forceful. You can be open and honest but still remain in con-trol of what the other side learns about you.

This happened in a negotiation that took place while the newspa-pers carried headlines that associated Donald Trump personally with the possible bankruptcy of the corporation that owned the Atlantic City casinos. The other side was skittish because they doubted Trump could meet the financial requirements of the transaction under con-sideration. While not denying the possible bankruptcy of the casino entity, Donald explained that it was less than 3 percent of his holdings. He agreed that it might be necessary to get relief from the 17.5 per-cent interest rate on the over $1 billion in bonds the corporation had issued. The outrageous interest payments were crippling the opera-tions. Still, a tough negotiating stance was required to solve the prob-lem. If the other side had done their homework, their degree of concern about Trump's financial condition might have been higher or lower. However, the fact that they believed what they read in the newspapers without further inquiry told us what tactics would work with these people down the negotiation road. While you are checking your assumptions and verifying what you know or believe about the other side remember, that it is a two-way street—they're doing the same thing but they'll do it in their own way. Sometimes as in this case, it is helpful to know what "their way" is.

BEWARE OF THE AURA OF LEGITIMACY

Of all the pitfalls that exist in any negotiation, *the aura of legitimacy* is far and away the worst one. I would classify all other pitfalls as pot-holes but I would list the aura of legitimacy as the Grand Canyon. Not only is it employed by charlatans, snake oil salesmen, con men, and other shady characters but also by reputable department stores, merchants, and lawyers. It's everywhere: "limited edition," "going out of business sale," "final markdown," "retail value $500—our price $250," "only 2 left" are but a few examples.

In case you're wondering why I included lawyers in the list, I must admit that I also use the "aura" in my real estate practice. The New York Real Estate Board distributes a form titled: "Standard form of Office Lease of the Real Estate Board of New York." It has a particular size, identifiable type, and is commonly used by real estate attorneys in New York. I prepared and had printed for my use a different version that looked the same as the NYREB form but I modified several clauses to make them more favorable to the landlords who were my clients. My form was titled: "Standard Form of Office Lease." I neither disclosed nor hid the fact that it was my specially tailored standard form. I can't recall how many lawyers representing tenants told their clients that my form was the standard form that they were thoroughly familiar with and accepted it without many changes. It worked so well that I developed two other versions of the Ross "standard form" specially adapted for different buildings. The "aura" worked because there is a general belief among all unskilled negotiators that things are really what someone indicates they are. If something is titled "Standard Form" they believe it is.

For example, an ad lists the price of a house at $400,000. Because it is right there in print, it has the aura of legitimacy. People often believe that that's close to the price needed to buy it. The truth is that the price indicated in the ad may bear little or no relation to the actual price the seller will accept. But the aura applies to everything. A major newspaper runs an article that real estate prices are dropping and cites a survey by a recognized authority as the basis for that conclusion. Unsuspecting readers believe the truth of the article because of the reputation of the newspaper. Without knowing the details of how the survey was conducted, they are willing to accept it as true—when in fact it may be a result of poor testing methods.

Looking behind the aura of legitimacy allows you to do two things. First, you are free to challenge what someone else has submitted in writing because you understand how the aura works to convince rather than question. Second, you can learn to use it as a very effective tool in any negotiation. For example, if you control the documentation and go into a negotiation using your documents, you have tremendous power. Your forms become the starting point of all subsequent discussions. You know what you put in and what you left out. The other side can only see what you put in. They have to figure out for themselves what you left out. Dealing with something you don't see is much more difficult. If you plan to be a skilled negotiator, you have to develop the ability to do both. The aura of legitimacy can work for you and to your advantage once you understand and realize its effectiveness or it can be extremely harmful if you don't recognize it. It's so important that I will revisit it later on.

IDENTIFY THE KEY PEOPLE INVOLVED IN THE NEGOTIATION

To negotiate effectively, you must identify the key people in the negotiation as well as their roles and motivations. Without that knowledge, you're operating in the dark. Are the decision makers even in the room? Have you spoken with them? These are critical questions that need to be answered before you commence any negotiation session. Some negotiations are carried out by using what I call: "messengers" or "spear carriers" and their roles and authority are very limited. Once you discover this, use them solely for the purpose of relaying your message to their superiors. *Never* negotiate with them in depth because they don't have the authority to make a final decision. At some point, you have to insist on talking directly to the person or persons who can make all major decisions. Sometimes key people may be in the room but they only listen. Find out who they are and why they're there. If the firm's chief accountant or general counsel is in attendance, he or she might not be directly participating in the negotiation, but the final deal might require a favorable nod from them.

When you go into a big negotiation, one that perhaps involves many people on each side—lawyers, accountants, experts, consultants—you need to be able to keep track of each person involved. Trump-style negotiation includes being very organized about gathering information about the people on the other side. In your first meeting make it a goal to learn the names and roles of those people with whom you'll be negotiating. Later on when you have more information, make notes and observations on the personal and professional life of the people you have to deal with. You can make some guesses about how they will function in the negotiation. As time goes on, you should refer to your notes and update them to reflect any changes or errors in your assumptions. In each session, you will learn more. Use the information you gather to determine the next steps in your negotiation strategy.

It's important to track the motives and perspectives of each person separately. Don't just think of the other side as having a single point of view. Each person involved in a transaction sees things from a slightly different angle, depending on his or her role in the big picture. If you're dealing with a real estate broker, you have to remember that he gets a commission for selling the house. He doesn't care if sellers get as much as they wanted or if you got it at the price you wanted to pay. He's not really interested in the terms, only that there is a deal. He will, however, try to stifle any effort on your part to ask for something that the seller will mostly likely reject. But when he relays your requests to the owner, he will try to convince the owner of the reasonableness of your requests. If, after this ping-pong game, you reach an impasse with the broker, you have to go around him and meet with the owner face-to-face. That's sometimes how a final agreement will be reached or the parties will go their separate ways. This is only one example, but the concept applies to every negotiation. The more you know about the people involved and what drives them, the better equipped you are to make effective arguments.

THREE THINGS YOU MUST LEARN
ABOUT THE OTHER SIDE

You can discover the other side's story as well as the motivations of each individual, by asking probing questions. You need to get a clear picture of the forces that control how each person negotiates. These include:

1. *Constraints.* There are all types of constraints: time, money, or reputation are but a few. Until you know the parameters under which the other side plans to operate, you don't really have a clear view of the playing field. And you can't win the game unless you know how the field is laid out, the rules of the game, and how the other side intends to play.

2. *Motivations.* Are people on the other side merely carrying out orders from above? Or do they see this particular negotiation as a career stepping-stone? Will they make a lot of money if the deal closes? You can discover these motivations by asking friendly questions such as: "How long have you been with the company? What's the scope of your job? If I make this deal are you going to sit on a beach in Cancun and drink piña coladas?" You find out much about people by expressing interest in them and what they will get out of a successful conclusion.

3. *Negotiating weaknesses.* These tell you a great deal. Here again, you can often uncover these with friendly and relatively inno-

cent questions. "Do you enjoy working in the corporate environment? Where do you see yourself going in the company? Are you authorized to make an actual decision in this? If we don't make a deal, how will that affect you personally?" Some people will literally lay their cards on the table, tell you the real deadline, price, terms they must take back with them, and what happens if they don't. If you're negotiating with someone who is easy to read, you might want to invite him to join your weekly poker party (just kidding). Meanwhile, ascertaining and evaluating his negotiation skills or weakness gives you a clear advantage in determining the final result.

Uncover Hidden Weaknesses and Information

If you are observant, you can pick up a lot of subtle signals and even discover hidden weaknesses from the other side. For example, a skilled salesperson might ask you a seemingly innocent question, "How soon do you need that new TV set?" You tell him you plan on having a Super Bowl party and want to watch the game on the new television with all your friends. You have displayed a weakness on your part that will be used against you in some way. The salesperson may switch you from what you'd like to what's available on such short notice. You are already at his mercy. It might mean he can talk you into spending more money than you anticipated, or buying a floor model or any other variation his fertile mind creates. The point is, you've given away information that you thought was of no value but it had tremendous value to the other side.

A different tactic might be to ask the salesperson, "What 50-inch HDTV have you got in stock that's a really good buy?" Now the ball's in his court. He says, "How much are you looking to spend?" You reply, "As little as possible." The negotiation continues but you haven't tipped your hand. That's how you should negotiate; throw the burden of fixing a price, setting the timing, and so on to the other side.

If you are observant, you can learn how people send signals without meaning to. A glance, a nervous habit, a change in voice pitch, looking at a spouse or coworker for approval or disapproval—all of these indicators give you valuable information.

Body language can reveal more than you mean to in a negotiation. One gentleman I knew liked to control the amount of time he spent in meetings. When he wanted to end the meeting, he would remove his wristwatch and place it on the table in between himself and the person talking. Without saying anything, he conveyed a clear message: Wind this up and let's end the meeting.

Usually people demonstrate weaknesses unintentionally by sending out subtle messages to the other side. If you watch and listen carefully, you'll learn much without saying a word.

If you are trying to figure out the other side's weaknesses, it often helps to ask oblique questions. Let's say you come to an impasse in the discussion of final price. You can ask a series of "what if" questions:

- "What if I paid all cash?"
- "What if I bought five pieces of equipment instead of two?"
- "What if I keep the Harley and sell you just the car?"

You can also uncover hidden information by asking timing questions, such as:

- "What if I wanted to close in six months?"
- "What if I paid 50 percent now and the balance next year?"

The answers to those questions could give you information that you can use in another area of the negotiation without asking a direct question that would lead to an untruthful answer.

Exploiting Weakness

Every negotiator wants to have an advantage. Once you uncover a weakness in the other side, exploit it while protecting yourself from exploitation of your weaknesses. To my knowledge, Donald Trump has no negotiating weaknesses except maybe the fact that he doesn't like to discuss minor details. He lacks the patience to work on unimportant paperwork, because he likes to focus on the big picture as a more productive usage of his time. That might be a weakness for others but for him it's just his way of doing business. He has his trusted, experienced staff to handle the details and discuss only the important items with him. This enables him to focus on many deals at the same time without getting bogged down in any one of them. Being a smart deal maker, Donald has learned to see the forest and let his subordinates see the trees. I think this is one of the keys to his success. Every good negotiator must learn when to delegate and when to do something himself. When in doubt, delegate.

Most negotiators don't have this same awareness of how to protect themselves from what could be perceived as a weakness or how to prevent the other side's way of doing business from frustrating the deal. Let's say one of your weaknesses is a tendency to talk too much about the details of a deal and you're negotiating with someone who thinks like Donald Trump—big picture, vision, future thinking. But you're aware that he doesn't have the patience for trivia. So when you start discussing detailed forecasts and pages and pages of numbers, you know what his reaction is likely to be.

You should curb your enthusiasm and say to him, "There are many minor details that I won't bore you with because your time is too valuable. Whom should I deal with in your organization who has the authority to get things done quickly?"

It's likely he will be relieved to hear you make this gesture. In reality, though, this gives you complete control over the documentation

47

and who will make the day-to-day decisions. You have uncovered the real deal maker for your transaction—and it's not the boss.

By the way, whenever it's necessary or smart to delegate something, you have to be able to trust the decision of your delegate. My relationship with Donald Trump is an excellent example of this. He trusts me. This is based on years of working together, but it also requires his willingness to delegate without micromanaging. He may be interested in only one aspect of a deal, but he trusts me to bring up with him anything that's important. I have to decide what would be important to him. We did one deal involving the negotiation of a long and complicated lease. I spent hours and days hashing out the details with the other side. Trump didn't get involved at all. When the whole lease was finalized, I took it to Trump and said, "Sign here."

Donald asked, "What's the rent?"

I told him, "I got $35 a square foot for 10 years from a strong tenant." Donald said, "That's great" and signed a lease that was over 100 pages long without reading it. He only wanted to know the rent he would receive. He knew—without any doubt—that if anything else in the lease was important I would tell him about it. He trusts people like me to protect his interests and to make sure he completes a deal within its appropriate time frame. I know he will never criticize me for minor things that were left out or included in the document. The key is that he knows if there is something important that he needs to know, I'll discuss it with him.

Two Common Weaknesses

There are a couple of other common weaknesses that I think you should be aware of. Maybe you have one or both of them but never perceived them as weaknesses. The first one is the inability to focus on details. Trust me when I say *the devil is in the details.* A vast majority of the populace accept fuzzy words and phrases by attaching their own meaning to them without recognizing the pitfalls. Here's what I mean. The words, "All customary fees and other charges are payable by the buyer" or similar language can be found in many documents. The words are so imprecise that in the event of a dispute, they could be subject to different interpretations depending on which side is doing the interpreting. How about the statement often seen on many contracts, "Subject to the usual conditions on the back?" Those curious enough to look at the small print on the back will find a list of items, most of which are unimportant. However, hidden among them could be a whopper that someone is trying to slip past you. Remember, "What the big print on the front giveth, the little print on the back taketh away!" If you want to be a successful negotiator, force yourself to read everything carefully. Conversely, there's nothing wrong with hiding something that's important to you but likely to be unacceptable to the other side in an inconspicuous place. If it's spotted and raised by the other side, discuss it normally; never plead guilty to using trickery.

The second weakness, which all novice negotiators share, is the inability to set and adhere to the time frames that are found in every negotiating situation. Every transaction starts at a specific time and builds momentum up to a date when it should either close or be abandoned. Unlike a sports game played in 60 minutes or a standard marathon of 26 miles, in negotiation you don't have a time clock or a finish line to guide you. Only experience can help you set a logical time frame but the pace and difficulties of negotiation often will force a revision. You have to fix the amount of time you're willing to spend on any transaction and take appropriate steps to see that the time allocation is not exceeded unless special circumstances warrant a finite overtime period. In another chapter, I show you how to accelerate or slow down a negotiation as the need arises.

4

BE A MASTER SALESMAN

*Create Bold Solutions to Problems
and Convince the Other Side
They're Getting More Than
They Ever Expected*

I F YOU APPROACH negotiation thinking your primary objective is *selling* your ideas and yourself, you will be far ahead of most people. It's common for people to focus on the numbers—price, income, expenses, monetary rewards—and to forget that many other issues beyond dollars are equally important.

In selling your ideas, you can't simply enter a room and start talking about what you want. You have to develop a strategy and have some idea of what you'd like to accomplish in every phase of the negotiation process and where you want to be at the end.

Perhaps the best example of a brilliant sales job was Trump's negotiation for his very first project, converting the empty run-down Commodore Hotel into what it is today, the Grand Hyatt at 42nd Street and Lexington Avenue in midtown Manhattan. If you consider the complexity of this deal, and that Trump was only 27 years old, you realize that it was an amazing sales job, not just to one person but also to numerous governmental entities, lenders, and political leaders.

It is important to understand the background during which this project took place in order to truly appreciate Trump's achievement. In 1974, New York was on the verge of bankruptcy and defaulting on its municipal bonds. Real estate was experiencing extensive vacancies, hotel occupancy was low, and foreclosures were everywhere. While most people saw these signs as good reasons to wait until things changed, Donald Trump saw this period of doom and gloom as a golden opportunity. The Commodore Hotel was dilapidated, vacant, and a blight in the heart of New York City and his idea—to transform it into a successful four-star hotel of 1,400 rooms—seemed grandiose and unrealistic to most people. In fact, when I met Donald for the first time, and he explained that this was the deal he wanted to pursue and how he planned to do it, I told him that I doubted he could make it happen because there were too many players—each with a different agenda. Trump thought otherwise, and asked for my help and negotiation guidance. Since I always relished accomplishing the seemingly impossible, I told him, "Count me in."

To make it work, Trump would have to bring together five different groups, each with its own interests and problems. These were Penn Central Railroad, which was bankrupt and owned the land under the Commodore Hotel and many other valuable properties on Park Avenue while it owed the city of New York $15 million in unpaid real estate taxes; New York City, which was also facing the possibility of imminent bankruptcy; the state of New York, which was struggling financially; a lender in possession of several defaulted loans in New York; a large hotel chain not intent on opening any new hotels given the sad state of New York tourism; and the current tenants in the building. The sheer number of parties, each with its own problems and interests at a time of turmoil, made the task of getting all of them to agree on their part of the transaction extremely arduous. I was especially pessimistic because any one of these groups could easily kill the deal if it refused to accept a role that it had never played before.

Donald is a great salesperson and championed his cause under the banner of revitalizing the city of New York. But to make the deal work, he was going to have to buy the Commodore Hotel at below market price, convince the railroad to deed the property to the New York State Urban Development Corporation for $12 million, and give the sale proceeds to the city of New York as partial payment of back taxes, convince the city that it was in its best interests to approve a long-term lease with the Urban Development Corporation that, as a governmental agency, would not be required to pay real estate taxes. The lease would provide the city with a minimal rental but included a share of profits from the operation of the hotel. The

Urban Development Corporation had to accept title in exchange for the $12 million that would be paid to the railroad, then for $12 million give Trump a long-term lease the city would approve *and* use its right of eminent domain to get possession of the building from all existing tenants. Trump also had to obtain a mortgage loan of at least $60 million to cover the cost of purchasing the land and renovating the hotel. But at this time, no bank was interested in adding another loan to its portfolio when it already had many defaulted loans subject to foreclosure. The hardest part of the negotiations was convincing the city that the $12 million it would get from the railroad, plus the monies it would receive from taxes on rooms, the benefits of creating jobs for several thousand workers, the revenues it would receive from returning tourists plus the profits from hotel operation were sufficient for the city to waive real estate taxes on the hotel.

As impossible as it seemed at the outset, Trump's personality, enthusiasm, and perseverance managed to overcome seemingly insurmountable obstacles. There were so many negotiations and renegotiations that the transaction took more than two years of hard work to complete. Just as an example, I prepared and negotiated 23 drafts of the lease that the city had to approve. Finally, with the full support of the mayor and with the governor behind the project, all of the pieces fell into place and the dream became reality. When the new Grand Hyatt did open in 1980, it led the way to a revitalization of the Grand Central Terminal area of New York; it also helped the city of New York to climb out of its near-bankrupt status and return to prosperity. The properties which the railroad owned on Park Avenue appreciated in value by reason of the revitalization of the city. By 1987, the hotel was reporting substantial operating profits in which the city shared. That year, Trump sold half of his interest in the property to the Hyatt Corporation for $85 million.

The qualities Donald Trump exhibited in negotiating this complex deal can be used as a model of the lengths you may have to go to sell yourself and the benefits of the deal to all others having an interest in the ultimate outcome.

ENTHUSIASM INSPIRES OTHER PEOPLE

If you start out thinking of yourself as a salesperson, you have taken the first step toward being an effective negotiator. Enthusiasm is always contagious, and if you demonstrate your enthusiasm it will inspire others, even people who think of themselves as your adversaries.

If Donald Trump had not been enthusiastic about his plans for the Commodore Hotel, he would never have convinced me to work with him. It was his enthusiasm that convinced all of the other parties to work with him. He was not enthusiastic only about what *he* would get from the deal. He truly believed everyone would benefit from working with him, especially his beloved city of New York. The strategy Donald conceived to sell himself and his ideas was to present a plan in which none of the parties involved could see how the idea could fail if they all agreed to play the role he outlined for them. Anyone who has worked with a governmental bureaucracy knows how difficult it is to get around the mind-set of "we don't do things that way." So, he had extensive feasibility studies made to convince the city of the severity of the current financial conditions and how his project could turn the whole problem around to the city's benefit. Trump was persuasive in his belief that the blighted midtown New York City area could be turned around only by new investments in real estate, improving conditions, and attracting tourism and business to return to the Grand Central area that is the heart of the city. Anyone who visits Grand Central Terminal and that area today realizes the reality of his vision; it worked. But back in the mid-1970s, few people had any faith in the city's ability to change conditions. Trump was able to foster changes through his unbridled enthusiasm.

Were it not for Trump's belief in his ideas, it would have fallen apart somewhere along the way. In fact, many complicated negotiations get bogged down and die on the vine because too many legal problems are raised, too many hurdles get presented, and too many negatives are voiced. The element missing in negotiations that fail is often personal enthusiasm and a key person's ability to sell the idea to the rest. This is where Donald Trump did his best work, keeping all of the interests at the negotiating table.

IF YOU BUILD RELATIONSHIPS WITH OTHER PEOPLE, IT MAKES THE DEAL WORK

I always tell people: The *money* is only part of any negotiation. Most people want to focus on their profit and they believe that if they successfully negotiate price everything else will fall into place, They're dead wrong; price is only one part of any deal. It is equally important to build a personal relationship as part of the negotiation process because you need the other side's help to conclude this transaction and all negotiations that flow from it. You *sell* yourself when you connect with the other person.

Donald Trump managed to move the Commodore Hotel project forward by investing his time in building relationships. This was essential. For example, the key decision maker at Penn Central Railroad was Victor Palmieri. Although Trump had never personally met the man, he telephoned him and asked for 15 minutes of his time. He got the meeting and in a short period of time convinced Palmieri that the railroad and the city would both win by signing on to the deal he envisioned. The two of them developed a solid working relationship, leading to Palmieri's help in convincing the city to cooperate with Trump. Remember, at the time of their first meeting, Trump had no track record, and Palmieri had no basis to believe in Trump's ability to complete the project. Trump built that relationship, convinced Palmieri they could work together, and thus gained an important ally.

Even if you're a small investor dealing with a small purchase—you can still use Trump's strategy to build your personal relationship with someone you need as part of a deal. For example, if you're going to need to get a loan approved to buy investment real estate, find the decision maker and connect with that person and expend the time and effort necessary to build the relationship. That will make it much easier to obtain a favorable decision. Instead of just another loan application represented by paperwork, you become a *known quantity* and a human being. This makes all the difference.

Whenever people enter a negotiation, there is a natural tendency to distrust what the other side says or does. When money is involved, people also suspect the other side's motives. If someone starts out saying, "I am going to help you make a lot of money," that often increases your suspicion because—again, as a starting point—you are inclined to *not* believe the other person.

Many negotiators think they have to make promises when they start to convince the other side, but in fact that is not the best way to begin. It's more important to develop a relationship, find some common ground, and get the other side to believe he is dealing with a person of integrity. Once you achieve this, you don't have to sell him the idea that you're going to help him make a lot of money. If you start by building the relationship and the trust, everything will fall into place.

An effective way to build a relationship is by starting your negotiation on the assumption that this will be the first of many deals and you intend to do more transactions with the other party down the road. Too many people want to proceed quickly through the negotiation with the idea of signing an agreement and then moving on to something else. But if you become known as a fair person, it creates positive experiences for all you come into contact with. If you ever deal with them again or with people they know, your reputation will precede you.

Showmanship Sells Your Ideas

The task in so many negotiations is to figure out how best to convey your ideas to people on the other side; convince them the ideas are sound and should be accepted at face value. This requires learning the basics of showmanship and by experimentation, learning what is most persuasive. Trump is known for his mastery of showmanship. This isn't just a matter of displaying detailed charts or eye-catching photographs, well-constructed and dramatic arguments, or an exaggerated sense of excitement. You have to understand that there is a fine line between hype and showmanship.

For example, Trump knew in the Commodore Hotel deal that since he was only 27 years old and with no real development experience, it was going to be a big challenge to persuade other parties of his capabilities and to obtain the millions of dollars in loans necessary to complete the undertaking. So he hired Henry Pearce, a well-respected New York real estate figure as an intermediary. One of his primary reasons for recruiting Pearce was to create the image of conventional wisdom and conservative values to the decision makers at governmental agencies and lenders alike. By having Pearce sitting by his side at the table while he negotiated and permitting the legendary, soft-spoken Henry Pearce to inject some wisdom he had gained from years of experience, Trump gave a major boost to the credibility of any idea he presented. Believing a 27-year-old with no experience is one thing. But with a well-respected member of the real estate community at his side, it created the added value of endorsement, and perhaps led others involved to believe that Pearce vouched for his abilities. Using Henry Pearce was a masterstroke of showmanship, not an example of hype.

Trump also knew that visible displays of showmanship would be required if he were to be successful in effectively showing the startling effect of transforming the dark and dingy Commodore Hotel into a new and modern flagship Grand Hyatt Hotel. He conceived of a new façade in glass and bronze in which the grandeur of Grand Central Terminal would be reflected, and he hired the renowned architect Der Scutt to create a visual masterpiece. He had several expensive detailed architectural renderings created to take to the mayor of New York City, knowing that it was going to be tough to convince him that he'd be able to turn a rundown eyesore into a modern luxury facility. He told Der Scutt to make the rendering and plans create the impression that a lot of money had been invested by Trump in the drawings alone. Trump knew that an impressive presentation by a famous architect would help in convincing skeptics. It worked. Showmanship paid off.

You don't have to hire an architect and draw up detailed sketches of your ideas to make effective use of showmanship. But if you're going to show a product or an idea to someone, a professional visual or audio presentation can help make the deal go through.

You also employ showmanship in a number of other ways. Dress appropriately to visit a lender, for example, to make the best possible impression. If you're negotiating with a big city bank for a loan, you should wear an expensive suit and a silk tie. Bankers will lend you more money if they think you don't need it. If you're meeting with someone on the golf course, wear appropriate clothes for that venue. Inquiring about apparel restrictions before you go can save you from embarrassment. First impressions are lasting impressions, so you have to carefully plan for the impression you want to make.

GOOD PREPARATION ULTIMATELY WINS THE DEAL

It is an extremely clever tactic to prepare so thoroughly for a negotiation that when you make your arguments they appear simple, compelling, and convincing. The other side doesn't need to know the hours of preparation you spent to be able to do that.

It always amazes me that so many people willingly go into a negotiation with little or no preparation. They don't do their research, develop an agenda, prioritize their arguments, or even think ahead to understand their goals before starting any meeting. If you are well prepared and the other side is not, guess who comes out better in the negotiation?

Donald Trump spends a great deal of time preparing himself and members of his team for every negotiation—not just for the big deals, but *every* negotiation he enters. He knows that by being as well prepared as they can be, there will be fewer surprises. He does not want to be caught off-guard by something that he hadn't considered and that could have been foreseen by better preparation. It is critical that he appears confident, that he has given a lot of thought to the entire transaction, and that he has the answers to any issues that may crop up. That sells him to the opposition.

If you're selling anything, you can use showmanship and preparation to anticipate what the potential buyer will relate to favorably. A comparison of price, benefits, or functions should be used to the extent they can be shown to give your product an advantage.

ZIFF'S PRINCIPLE OF LEAST EFFORT

A researcher named Ziff performed an extensive negotiation experiment that led him to conclude that most people will extend the least amount of effort required from them in any negotiation in which they are involved. This tells you all you need to know about the best way to proceed in every negotiation. Ask yourself, "If I were in their shoes, What would I want?" or "What questions would I want answered?" Come up with satisfactory answers to those questions before you even begin your discussions and Ziff's principle takes over from there. You will have lulled them into a false sense of security and they're willing to take it from there without verifying the accuracy of what you said.

At the appropriate time, the Trump team simplifies things for people during a negotiation. He has the knack of explaining to his negotiators the best way of cutting to the chase by careful preparation. For example, when he wants to get investors interested in investing with him in a transaction, he has his financial people crunch the numbers using several different scenarios. He picks the one he likes best and that is used as the basis of a summary for investors. Then he writes in big letters at the bottom of the page, "Return on your money: 20 percent a year." Since that's in Donald's distinctive handwriting, most readers focus on that 20 percent, paying very little attention to the details. But Trump's instincts also tell him that too many details could turn people off because it could lead to the feeling, "This deal is just too complicated for me." Ziff's principle tells him that people are primarily interested in the bottom line. Get them there as soon as you can and they're sold. Intelligent preparation properly presented can move other people from "maybe" to "yes." If they want to go back later and check the numbers themselves, or hand it to their financial advisor, that's easily done because the Trump team has already done the preparation. But Trump's statement at the bottom of the page is what is important. When and if he brings an advisor in, he tells the advisor, "Look into the numbers but I really like the deal."

I utilized my knowledge of Ziff's principle to create a windfall for one of my clients. He was building a new building and said it would help his financing if he could demonstrate a fixed annual cash flow rather than one that fluctuated depending on the amount of real estate taxes payable by the owner in any year. He wanted to know if I could solve his problem. The typical lease clause provided that a tenant would pay its share of tax increases over the taxes paid by the owner in the first year after the term of the lease commenced. I said I would draft a new clause and figure out how to sell it to the tenants' attorneys who had never seen such a provision before. The owner wanted to limit his tax liability for the building to $6.00 per square foot. Knowing that the tenants' attorneys would question that number, I had a survey made of the amount of taxes per square foot paid by owners of comparable buildings in the area. My review of over 30 buildings disclosed that the amount of taxes per square foot averaged between $5.00 and $6.50 per square foot. I prepared a list that identified 15 buildings where the taxes were $5.50 a square foot or less. When I was questioned about fairness of the new concept, I showed this tailored list to the tenants' attorneys and said that their client was getting a break by not paying anything until the taxes exceeded $6.00 a square foot because my statistics showed an average for buildings in the area of $5.00 to $5.50 per square foot. Now here's where Ziff's principle came in. I doubted that the opposition would take the time and effort to make its own independent study and I was right. Knowing that they would be skeptical of my statement, I carefully identified each building on my tailored list as to address, size, and age and the tax rate per square foot. Anyone examining my handiwork would attest to its accuracy. So every tenant's attorney told his or her client that my concept really gave them a tax break. Later on, when the city set the initial tax rate at $10.00 a square foot, the same attorneys had to explain an immediate $4.00 per square foot increase in rent to their clients. Had they really done their homework, they might have avoided the embarrassment.

In all negotiations, you should prepare yourself by knowing as many facts and gathering as much information as you can prior to entering the negotiation arena. For example, if you're planning to buy a home, you need to know what similar properties in the area you're interested in have sold for in the past month or two. If you're thinking of buying a new car, go on the Internet to learn the dealer's cost. Do your homework and it will pay off handsomely. Don't let Ziff's principle work against you. Be the rare person willing to carefully investigate the completeness of all information you receive.

You Must Have Tenacity to Succeed

You'll never hear someone complain that he went through a transaction but the other person was "too tenacious." He may express grudging admiration for the other person for sticking to their plan, pursing their goal, or closing the deal. But tenacity is never viewed as a negative trait. If you really want to sell yourself and your ideas, you have to be tenacious.

If Donald Trump had not been tenacious for two years, the Commodore Hotel deal would never have gone through. It required a determination that most people would not have been willing to invest and a tenacity that most people do not see any necessity to develop in themselves. But if you want to really succeed, tenacity is an absolute requirement. If you give up easily, you simply won't get there.

In fact, Donald Trump's biggest successes grew out of difficult negotiating situations in which his tenacity made the difference. He has been able to get bargain prices on properties because their problems were viewed as insurmountable by everyone else. His tenacity, combined with his ability to identify what people could be expected to do to make the deal successful, allowed him to forge his way through those difficulties.

In the early part of the Commodore Hotel negotiations, the city was concerned about who would operate the hotel that Trump had in mind. They voiced a valid concern: What did Donald Trump know about profitably running a first-class hotel? The answer was, he knew nothing about how to run a hotel. This was a major roadblock for Trump. Without a recognized hotel operator, the city wasn't interested in his proposal. So Trump used all his negotiating skill to convince Hyatt to manage the hotel for him. After Hyatt learned what a rich deal Trump had created, they insisted on becoming a 50 percent owner. Hyatt was the last important link in the chain. With Hyatt as operator, a lender felt comfortable in funding the project and the city was satisfied that the monies it would receive from the lease would be substantial.

To be successful in a negotiation, you have to expend the amount of time and effort necessary to sell yourself and your ideas. While it is unlikely that any of your transactions will be remotely as complex as Trump's Commodore deal, the basic ideas—showmanship, enthusiasm, preparation, use of Ziff's principle of least effort, coupled with unbridled tenacity can successfully turn any negotiation to your advantage.

5

CONTROL THE PACE
OF THE NEGOTIATION

*Use Timing, Deadlines, Delays, and
Deadlocks to Your Advantage*

Getting pulled into a quick deal is always a mistake. It might be a good deal, but the speed and pace of the negotiation should be *your* decision, based on your agenda and negotiating strategy and not the other side's. Trump understands this principle better than anyone. When he was negotiating to buy 40 Wall Street, he was continually frustrated in his dealings with the owner's U.S. agent. If the deal was going to happen, he knew he had to fly to Germany to establish a working relationship with the owner, the patriarch of a respected and wealthy German family. He needed to convince the owner to amend the ground lease. Trump sought a lease flexible enough to let him perform major renovations and also to convert part of the building to residential use if desired. Working against him and this visionary idea was the building's troubled history. It had been mismanaged for years, gone through bankruptcy, and had poor business and cash flow results. Trump did his research on the owner and assumed that the German owner, a multimillionaire named Walter Hinneberg, would welcome the chance to escape the management headaches of operating a 90 percent vacant office building in New York City. Trump wanted to persuade him that he would be a good tenant who would enhance the value of the property, by undertaking a major renovation and restoring the building to its past grandeur. So Trump prepared numerous pictures and plans to demonstrate how he intended to turn the building into a showcase that would make the owner proud.

You would think that anyone anxious to embark on an ambitious project like this would want a quick deal, but Trump knew in this situation—with the complexity of renegotiating a lease with an absentee

66

owner who had several bad experiences with prior tenants—that he needed to move slowly and carefully to establish a rapport and trust with his counterpart. Hinneberg was impressed that Trump flew all the way to Germany to meet with him, and from the first meeting on they connected well. Because he was still compelled to negotiate through Hinneberg's New York representative, Trump knew it would be a long drawn-out battle before he got what he needed. It took Trump nearly a full year to get the deal structured in an acceptable manner—including the creation of a revised ground lease with a rent abatement during the period of renovation, and the flexibility Trump needed while fully protecting the interests of the land owner. If he had tried to rush the deal, it probably would never have reached a successful conclusion.

CONTROL THE PACE

A quick negotiation also often ends with one side feeling unhappy. Inevitably someone overlooks a critical detail. It shouldn't be you, Also, by rushing, it's likely that you will not get the best deal available because you haven't had a reasonable opportunity to explore all the possibilities. Another reason it makes sense to go slowly is that a successful negotiation involves satisfying the "ego requirement" of both sides, and that takes time. This means you need to be able to spend time with the other side and express genuine interest in them and what will satisfy them. If you rush, it sends the opposite message, namely that you have no interest in them personally but are only interested in the deal. Investing time with others in a negotiation imparts a genuine impression that you really care about hearing the other person's ideas and trying to satisfy his or her desires. Also, it gives you the chance to pick up useful information. When you ask questions, gather background information, and get to know them, you find out about their motivations, interests, and goals—all part of their "ego." All of this helps you to negotiate with them more effectively and to reach a mutually satisfying outcome.

This does not mean you should never pick up the pace. There are many instances where you have a great advantage in moving the process along, especially if you see the other side is weakened by going slowly. When this happens, the worst thing you can say is "get back to me when you can." The smart thing to do is to pick up the pace. Tell the other side, "I need the answer in two days or I will go somewhere else for what I want."

Now, let's look at the reverse situation. What if the other side comes to you and demands an answer in two days. With them trying to rush you, it probably makes sense to slow everything down. You could ask, "Why two days? I'm busy working on other things so I won't be able to give you an answer for a week or so. Is that okay?" You don't refuse the two-day deadline; you are determining if it's based on reality or if it is arbitrary. If it is the latter, a longer time frame will be acceptable.

The tactic—speeding up when the other side wants to move slowly, or slowing down when they want to move faster—is not simply a means of gaining control for its own sake. There is a specific reason for such actions. When I take control, it gives me an opportunity to analyze how the other side responds to my change of pace. The degree of control I exercise or attempt to exercise, and the other side's response to it, reveals a great deal about the strength or weakness of their position or their negotiating skills, but gives away nothing about my position or my pattern of negotiation.

I always analyze the response I get when I try to speed up or slow down a negotiation. Did they quickly agree? Were they upset? Did they accept my suggestion with a "fine" or "no problem?" Did they exhibit frustration? What I find out gives me good information about my adversaries. Speed up the negotiation, or slow it down, depending on which speed works to your advantage at a particular time. But if in doubt, go slowly.

THREE EASY WAYS TO CONTROL THE PACE OF A NEGOTIATION

I use three guiding rules when it comes to controlling the pace of a negotiation. They are:

1. *Don't accept any offer right away.* Hold back on acceptance. Remember, satisfaction is necessary for both sides and, ironically, when people get something too easily, it isn't satisfying. It makes them think they could have gotten more if they tried harder and that thought is troubling.

   One of the foundational principles of a successful negotiation is that you must create satisfaction in the minds of your adversaries, You want someone to come through a negotiation with you and conclude, "It was tough—very difficult—but I got what I wanted and I did a great job getting it." That is satisfaction. It takes a lot of time and a lot of give and take. But it pays off at the end.

2. *Do be indecisive.* By this, I mean that there are times in the negotiation where indecision can be used as a tactic for controlling the pace. By saying, "I don't know about that. Let me think it over and I'll get back to you." You have delayed reaching an agreement, and you maximize what I call the *invested time principle.* Simply stated, this means that the more time people spend in a transaction, the less likely they are to walk away from it. Time invested enhances the desire to make it end successfully.

   People naturally hate spending time without reaching the ultimate conclusion. So you can use your indecision as a way to get more time-consuming information from the other side thus increasing the other side's investment of time, money, or both. In a very real sense, time invested in negotiation feels the same as money invested in the market. You want the final payoff. You don't want to just get up and walk away empty handed.

3. *Don't do quick negotiations.* I can't emphasize enough the importance of this. In any quick deal, one side gets an inferior deal. Trump-style negotiation is aimed at creating satisfaction for both sides, not a short negotiation where one side wins and the other side loses.

   If you have no alterative but a quick negotiation, it is critical that you be far better prepared and that you know more than the other side. This is the only way to protect yourself from the disadvantage of a short fuse. If you do a quick negotiation, you are not going to achieve the feeling of mutual satisfaction that leads to long-term trust and friendship that leads to smooth negotiations in the future.

DEADLINES

It is always desirable to be able to control the pace, but there may be instances where a deadline exists that can't be changed. Of course, if you know the other side is operating under a fixed deadline and wants to make a deal, you gain control of the negotiation by delaying an agreement until they feel the pressure of the approaching deadline. If you disagree on an important deal point, try to wait until the last possible minute to resolve it. Unskilled negotiators have a tendency to cave in at that time. The general feeling people have as a deadline approaches is, "I must accomplish something now." This feeling of frustration, however, can easily lead people into making a concession they might otherwise reject.

People don't like deadlines because that is when they feel the most vulnerable. The deadline is a form of pressure, and few people make good decisions under pressure. But remember, if the deadline is suffered by the other side, they are at a disadvantage. *They* feel the need to meet the deadline, *you* don't. Of course you want to conclude the deal, but giving the other side the deadline gives you a negotiating advantage.

Years ago, I read about an experiment done by a researcher studying people's tendencies in negotiations. He set up a series of mock negotiations to which he invited people in different walks of life to apply for the right to participate for a modest fee and a free meal. Before the beginning of the negotiation session, he divided the participants who had various levels of negotiation skills into two groups. The scenario involved a pharmaceutical company that had introduced a new drug that had a number of serious side effects such as loss of equilibrium, loss of sight, and possibly eventual blindness.

In this mock negotiation, half of the negotiators represented claimants who were suing the company for injuries they had suffered from using the drug. They were told the average settlement sought from the drug company was $1 million. The remaining participants were to represent the drug company and try to get the claimant to accept the lowest possible cash settlement. Each side was told they had exactly one hour to reach a negotiated settlement. They were told that a bell would ring every 10 minutes, followed by an announcement of the time remaining. During the last 10 minutes, the bell and announcement would take place every minute. If no settlement was reached by the end of the allotted hour, the parties would be considered hopelessly deadlocked. After the mock negotiation was over, the participants were required to fill out a detailed questionnaire and the answers were analyzed by the team conducting the experiment.

One of the interesting conclusions reached as a result of this experiment was that approximately 90 percent of all settlements were reached in the final five minutes. This verified what I had previously concluded from my own experience: People have a tendency to wait until some deadline is about to expire, but they want to make the deal happen. Inability to agree is tantamount to failure in most people's mind, and coming to an agreement—even one not as good as you wanted—is a form of success.

Now that you know how deadlines affect unskilled negotiators here are four guidelines you should adopt as part of your negotiation portfolio:

1. *People typically wait until deadlines to reach an agreement.* One reason is the desire to make a deal; the other reason relates to the invested time philosophy. People hate to think that the time they have already expended in a negotiation has been wasted.

2. *Every transaction will meander unless there is a compelling reason to consummate it or kill it.* Without some compelling reason to reach total agreement, the discussions will just go on and on, with no pressure to reach a resolution. But at some point, things have to get resolved. You will need to take steps to push for resolution when it's to your advantage to do so. Until then do what you can to induce the other side to spend a great deal of time and money in pursuit of a settlement, but keep the expenditure of your team to a minimum lest you yourself might fall prey to the invested time principle.

3. *The worst deadlines are those imposed by your side.* Some people think that placing a deadline on the outcome of a negotiation gives them control; the exact opposite is true. The party with the deadline is the one under pressure; the other party has the advantage.

   With this in mind, try to prevent people on your side from setting any deadline for you in your negotiation. Never let the other side know you have a deadline unless the disclosure will cause them to reach the solution you desire. If you wish to put pressure on the other side by increasing the speed of the negotiation, give the other side an imaginary deadline. You can change it at will.

4. *Test all deadlines to see if they are real or fictitious.* Some people will come into a negotiation with you and say, "This deal has to be finished by the end of the week, or forget it." Your job is to test its validity. You might respond by saying, "Unfortunately, I have to be out of town for the next 10 days, why can't it wait until I return?"

   If the other side wavers, the deadline they declared is obviously fictitious. If they have a logical explanation as to why the deadline is necessary, you have learned something of value. Maybe it's time to head home and see whether they let you go. You should also test all deadlines imposed by your side. If the president of your company sends you into a negotiation saying "I need an answer within 48 hours," you can ask, "Why is such a short timeframe necessary?" The validity of his explanation will be your guide whether to either accept it or question it further.

A VALUABLE NEGOTIATION TOOL: YOUR CRITICAL PATH

In every negotiation that you're involved with, it's important for you to create your own *critical path*. The critical path starts with the date the negotiation begins and ends on a date, let's call it the "outside date," that you reasonably anticipate the negotiation should end successfully or be aborted. For planning purposes, it's very helpful to scope out the individual milestones and the steps needed to get there, in appropriate order, indicating the estimated time each will take. Once a real deadline enters the negotiation, that deadline becomes the "outside date."

For example, I have a car and the lease runs out December 31. I have to get either another car or extend the lease by that date. So December 31 is my outside date. Next I look at today's date. Assume it's January 1 therefore I have 12 months before the outside date to complete my quest. Before I start serious negotiations, I have to know what I want in a new car. I think I don't need more than a month to do that. The sales incentives traditionally start in June, so my anticipated start date for my critical path is May 1. When I have to concentrate on what features I want in a new car so I start serious negotiations by June 1.

Before that date, there is preliminary work to do. I research costs and comparative values. I have to decide which dealerships I am going to visit. I must narrow down the models and makes I like and decide how much I am willing to spend. If this is going to take longer than 30 days, the start date for my critical path should be earlier than May 1.

Assuming I successfully negotiate the purchase of a new car, how soon before the outside date must the negotiation be completed so that the timing will work with my plans for my present car? If I intend to give it back to my leasing company concurrently with buying or leasing a new car from them, the timing is easy. If, however, I decide to buy or lease a new car from another dealer, the timing is more complicated. Because creating a viable *critical path* requires separate consideration of possible alternatives, I may have to create different critical paths for each scenario. Learning how to create the critical path organizes your thinking about the steps you need to take to complete a given task. It takes some serious and careful thinking to construct a critical path. Mastering the art of creating a critical path is an essential attribute of every skilled negotiator.

DELAYS

In addition to dealing with deadlines that invariably arise in a negotiation, you should also know that unanticipated delays will inevitably occur. I use delay tactics whenever it's to my advantage to do so. But if you're keeping an eye on your critical path throughout the negotiation, as you should be, what happens if the other side tries to delay things? That's when you have to build a "fire" under them to get them to move faster. The fire can be a reduced price, a loss of the deal, or a change in the timing they want. When I use delay, it's just another tactic. For example, if I think that the other side has a dire need for money, I will slow down the pace. When I do, the other side might complain and tell me they really need the money quickly. This gives me a chance to renegotiate by trading speed for money. If the other side really can't live with the delay, their only choices are to give me something to get things to speed up once again or threaten to walk away from the deal. Every negotiation has an invisible timeline. It starts, meanders for a period of time, and either builds to a successful conclusion or aborts. After you have obtained the extensive experience that comes with having many negotiations, you will develop a gut feeling as to whether the negotiation is proceeding in a timely and appropriate fashion toward your intended goal.

PLANNING A NEGOTIATION

Often delays occur because there are several people involved in the negotiation and the schedule of one critical person makes him unavailable on a certain date. If you don't know this beforehand, avoiding the delay is beyond your control. You should ascertain the schedules of all participants in advance to avoid delays that good planning could have eliminated. If necessary, either move the deadline back or get the missing person to give authority to someone else to finish the deal.

All negotiating tactics aside for the moment, a delay caused by poor planning is simply disorganization. It frustrates everyone, can cost money, and may even kill the deal. So whenever you are in a multiparty negotiation, constantly identify any scheduling problems. This will affect the way that both sides negotiate; it could also be used as an opportunity for you to speed up or slow down the discussion.

USE PARALLEL NEGOTIATING TRACKS

There is rarely a single right answer or outcome in a negotiation. Most of the time, many workable solutions can be found if you look for them. Creating a parallel negotiating track plan B in addition to plan A, which you are already negotiating, will make it more likely that you reach a satisfactory outcome. You can propose a parallel track for an alternative deadline or price or any other important part of a deal. I previously compared a $500,000 price payable in 90 days with a $400,000 price payable now. This is a parallel track combining a closing date with price. You may see similar arrangements in real estate transactions. A buyer might negotiate with a seller, saying, "I'll give you full price if you pay my closing costs" or a furniture buyer may tell the salesperson, "I'll agree to pay this much if you promise delivery tomorrow—and you waive the normal delivery charge."

The great thing about parallel tracks is that they let you open up many different solutions rather than taking a simple "that's the price, take it or leave it" approach. It also fits nicely with a well thought-out critical path. Parallel tracks are the critical path variations that will make a deal viable from several different viewpoints.

Murphy Was an Optimist

You remember Murphy's Law, of course—"Anything that can go wrong will go wrong at the worst possible time." This applies to negotiations.

A delay might come from either side for any number of reasons, or it may be imposed on both sides by an outside factor. For example, you're negotiating to buy a house. You and the seller have reached an agreement: You've agreed on the closing date and when you will move in. The seller has an investment opportunity and needs your cash from the purchase. Suddenly the house burns to the ground. This is an example of a Murphy's Law event that may kill the deal or, at the very least, result in a change of some of the terms. There is no way to adequately anticipate the unexpected, but if you have taken the time to establish a relationship of mutual trust the parties will work things out no matter what unseen force has intervened.

Use Deadlocks to Your Advantage

What is a deadlock? A deadlock occurs when the parties cannot agree on some element under discussion and they cease negotiating. The general public and unskilled negotiators have an innate fear of deadlocks and you will find examples of this in almost every negotiation. They think a deadlock is tantamount to failure, and they're terrified of failure. However, deadlocks can always be broken and I'll show you how. Knowing that you can break a deadlock at will, you can use your opponent's fear of deadlocks to your advantage. If one party is willing to accept a deadlock at a point in time, that party has a distinct advantage in the negotiation process. When you express a willingness to cease negotiating because of a disagreement between the parties, you put a lot of pressure on the other side. What most people don't realize is that deadlocks can be broken and there's always a way to reopen discussions.

There are several reasons you might want to initiate a deadlock. First, it shows your determination and confidence in your position to the other side. Second, it tests whether the other side has the same determination and confidence in their position. Third, it determines whether any additional concessions may be available from the other side to get you to forego the deadlock, Fourth, deadlock shows others on your side that it might be the "end of the road" (a demonstration that you've achieved everything possible and there's no more to be won). And fifth, a deadlock creates a change of pace, which may enhance your degree of control over the negotiation.

Deadlocks are useful because they display the position of the other side and freeze them at that point. So I might say to my adversary, "If you don't agree to pay the $10,000, there is no deal and I'm out of here." If the other side stands firm, I must leave. The negotiation is not necessarily over because deadlocks can be broken. But I have learned that the other side is willing to let the deal go for the sake of $10,000. It clarifies my position and also theirs.

If the other side is operating on a time constraint, to them a deadlock is a disaster. So if you're willing to set up a deadlock, you're holding a far better hand because the other side has to do something because of their timeframe. They can let the deal die and ignore the emotional and monetary costs of their invested time or make some additional compromise that will get you to modify your stance.

If *you* initiate a deadlock as a strategy, always smile and be pleasant as you do it. Just tell the other side that you just can't do what they request. This leaves an opening to save face if you want to come back later and change your position. For example, you deadlock a deal because you think you can get a better deal from someone else. If you find out later that the first deal offered was the best you could find, you want to be able to go back and reopen negotiations with the first party. Never burn your bridges by saying something like, "I wouldn't make a deal with you if you were the last person on earth." Instead, say something like, "Think it over and if you change your mind, call me." A parting gesture like that leaves the door open if you wish to return.

Creating a deadlock can work to your advantage if you are being second-guessed by somebody on your side. For example, let's say you want to buy a house and after negotiation the seller wants $400,000 dollars and you think that's the best price you can get. But what if your wife says, "I think the seller will take $350,000."

So I tell the seller, "$350,000 is my best offer."

The seller says, "I told you I wanted $400,000 and I won't take less. If that's not acceptable to you, I'll sell it to somebody else."

Now I have tested the strength of the seller's position; and my wife is now convinced that $400,000 is the price to be paid if she wants the house.

Big Organizations Dread Deadlock

It gives you a great negotiating advantage to realize that when you're talking to a big company, a deadlock works in your favor. Most people believe that the bigger company has all of the negotiating advantages, but it doesn't. Before any large company decides to do a deal, many layers of approval are required. The company is like a huge ocean liner; once it starts steaming in one direction it's hard to turn around. The big company hates deadlock because it stalls the fulfillment of the deal that its executives have approved and requires reconvening all people involved in the decision-making process. It ties up people and prevents an approved deal from moving forward. By using this knowledge in a negotiation, you will often be able to gain concessions from larger, richer, more influential negotiators—simply because they find it embarrassing to explain to their managers why the deal is in disarray.

For example, a large corporate developer is planning to build a subdivision and you hold two lots in a key location. The developer has been able to work out deals with all of the other landowners in the area at attractive prices. But you know that once the infrastructure of roads and utilities are in place, all of the land in the area will be much more valuable. Even though a tentative agreement was reached as to price, you create a deadlock by demanding more money for your lots. You deadlock is effective because you know the developer is working on deadlines from the city, with subcontractors and suppliers, as well as lenders and your lots are an important part of the planning process. If you hold firm, you will undoubtedly have the opportunity to negotiate a better deal for yourself, but a word of caution—be careful not to overplay your hand.

Ways to Break a Deadlock

You can always break a deadlock, even though people tend to think the existence of a deadlock means the deal is off. This isn't so. As you will learn, you can break a deadlock in several different ways.

First, by postponing a decision on the item that caused the deadlock and attacking other issues. For example, you could say, "Assuming we can agree on the price, what else is open?" Usually the other side is willing to sidestep a thorny problem and focus on the other ones that are much easier to resolve. If so, you're back on the track of a friendlier negotiation. After you've gotten the minutia out of the way, it's appropriate to say, "Well, we reached agreement on everything else let's agree on the price." The hostility that surrounded a deadlock has vanished and there is a favorable environment for creating an acceptable agreement of the remaining issue. If you want to break a deadlock, start by talking about anything but the issue that created the deadlock.

Second, you can make one or more minor concessions to the other side and ask them to reciprocate. Any further discussion restarts the negotiation.

Third, go "off the record" and try to open up an avenue of resolution with people at a different or a higher level. Since they were not there at the time the deadlock happened, they might be predisposed to act as a peacemaker.

Breaking a deadlock consists primarily in defusing the ego, temper, and dug-in-heels approach that is so easy to fall into during the competitive phase of the negotiation. If you understand human nature, you won't have too much difficulty in figuring out how to end a deadlock. The next chapter provides even more information about human nature and how to harness it to improve your negotiating success.

6

HARNESS THE POWER OF HUMAN NATURE

Psychological Negotiating Tactics

Human nature ultimately determines how deals come together or fall apart. So understanding human nature is essential to understanding negotiation. Once people form bonds and become friends—or arrive at an impasse and become enemies—it is virtually impossible to change.

In Chapter 1, I told you about the rapport that was created between Donald Trump and Leonard Kandell when Kandell granted the lease Donald needed to build Trump Tower. Leonard Kandell liked my work on that deal and became my client from the day it concluded until he died many years later. In 1987, I had left the active practice of law and was no longer representing Donald. To complete Trump Tower, Donald needed a favor from Kandell. I was in the peculiar position of being Kandell's lawyer and Trump's ex-lawyer. Donald needed an easement from Kandell to permit a column supporting Trump Tower to go partially onto Leonard's property, so Donald asked me to get him that easement. Leonard asked me, "George, does the easement really affect me?" and I said, "Not really; it permits Trump to install a column 32 feet below grade and the column straddles the property line." Kandell replied, "Donald's always been fair with me so go ahead and give him the easement." So for no charge Kandell gave Donald the easement that he needed.

Not long after that, Donald called me again and said "I have to move the column further into Kandell's property. Can you get me Leonard's permission to do so?"

The sketch that Donald sent me disclosed that instead of straddling Kandell's property line, the new location of the column would place it totally on Kandell's property, which was a big difference.

When I told Kandell what Donald Trump wanted, he said, "George, if I wanted to, I'm sure I could get Donald to pay me a million or two for this right. But he's always been a gentleman and I'm satisfied with my dealings with him. Give Trump the easement for nothing."

Kandell's belief was correct. To satisfy my own curiosity, I told Donald, "I can get you the easement but it will cost you $2.5 million; is that okay?" In his typical negotiating style, Trump said, "George, I don't really need that column there so for $2.5 million I'll put it elsewhere." I replied, "Donald, this is George you're talking to and I know that the city is insisting that you widen your proposed atrium. I also know that the column you are planning to put on the easement supports the entire corner of your building. We both know how much you need it." After much discussion, Donald reluctantly said he would pay the $2.5 million. That's when I told him Kandell was willing to give the easement to him for nothing. The point is that the relationship established between Kandell and Trump transcended the normal relationship of neighbors, real estate investors, and business negotiators. Their relationship was based on friendship and trust.

Kandell took this level of trust even further. He also owned the land at 112 Central Park South in Manhattan. The land was subject to a long-term lease that was owned and controlled by a man named John Coleman. Kandell had many disputes with Coleman and felt he could not be trusted. Kandell told me, "George, I'd like to make Donald my watchdog so that if there's ever a problem with Coleman, Donald will be the one to fight my battles and protect my interest and those of my children and grandchildren."

In exchange for Donald's agreement to act as Kandell's watchdog, Leonard gave Donald an interest in the rental the property would generate when the lease was subject to renewal. Trump was entitled to 15 percent of the amount by which the renewal rent exceeded the prior rent. The point here is simply that, based on a long-standing relationship between Kandell and Trump, Kandell knew he could trust Donald to be honest and to protect his heirs. Kandell was always willing to pay for what he got and in this case he bought peace of mind.

Because human nature plays a major role in every transaction, Donald Trump usually begins a negotiation by speaking to the other side, and trying to learn what is important to them. Once he has identified their desires, he tries to address them. As long as both sides get something they can live with, the negotiation is successful. That is at the core of Trump-style negotiation.

The most important aspect to negotiation is that everybody has to come out with an acceptable degree of satisfaction. You have to figure out the best way to accomplish that. If you satisfy the other side, you get satisfaction as well.

Psychology of Negotiating

The first thing you need to know about the psychology of negotiating is that it's easy to sell something unique or different. This is the *aura of exclusivity*, that I discussed earlier. You should work to create it in the minds of others. It doesn't matter what you have to sell, your success rests on your ability to create and maintain this aura. You will be in a far stronger position if you offer something the other side cannot get elsewhere.

This works in every kind of transaction. If you're trying to land a job, sell a house, or buy a refrigerator—all of these situations can be improved by conveying your own aura of exclusivity, namely your ability to convince the people that you are dealing with that you have exactly what they want. Remember and observe the rules we discuss next.

People Want What They Can't Have or What Somebody Else Wants

The greed and envy motive is alive and well in most people. Recall the lesson from the classic movie *Citizen Kane* in which an incredibly wealthy man virtually destroys his entire life because of one small thing he didn't get as a child. You can learn a lot from that.

If you really want to get customers, put up a sign, "just sold." The effectiveness of an auction depends on the number of bidders. The more frenzied the bidding becomes, the more each bidder thinks, "If so many others want it, I've got to buy it." When an opportunity arises to create an auction atmosphere, grab it.

People Become Overwhelmed When Faced with Too Many Decisions

You can actually prevent someone from making a decision by giving him too much information or too many things to consider all at once. Complexity frightens people and the most common reaction to fear is to flee. If someone is forced to make too many decisions at one time, he might choose not to make any at all. It's like trying to get someone to swallow a pill the size of a golf ball. If you gave it to her all at once, she would choke on it. But if you break it into tiny pieces and gave it to her a little at a time over a long period, she will swallow the whole dose and never realize it. In your negotiating game plan, try to determine the best time to seek a decision on each item under discussion and raise it at the appropriate time. If you're negotiating at a leisurely pace you can hide the tough stuff among the no-brainers.

People Succumb to the Aura of Legitimacy

Here is a more intensive examination of the almost hypnotic effect of this phenomenon—the aura of legitimacy—that I discussed earlier.

It is possible to say something that's entirely false, but if you say it with authority as if you believe it yourself, or better yet if it is printed on an official looking piece of paper, that creates an aura of legitimacy that people believe. The bigger the lie and the stature of the teller, the more it's accepted. What better example is there than how we, the American people, believed it when we were told by President Bush and others that Saddam Hussein had weapons of mass destruction, was a sponsor of terrorism, and that immediate action was required to protect the United States? Congress and the American people fell for it hook, line, and sinker. It took three years, thousands of lives, and billions of dollars before the truth was known. But *everything seemed legitimate*. Let's look at other examples that people run into every day.

For example, let's say you're in a store and you see a sales ticket: "Retail value $500—our price $350." You think you're saving $150 so that's a good deal. But where did that price of $500 come from? Who dreamed that price up? It seems legitimate because it's there in writing and people have a tendency to believe the truthfulness of what they read. The written word has the aura of legitimacy.

Let's say you read an article in a major newspaper. You tend to believe it because, well, it was in the *Times*. But in reality it's only an interpretation or the slant given the story by the columnist or reporter. Even with the many revelations of wrongdoing at major newspapers, we still tend to believe whatever we see in those papers. This is the real power of the press.

The same phenomenon works with television. "It was on television so I believe it." Well, the fact is that you are mesmerized by the "aura." What you hear is very rarely the whole truth, and may even be entirely misleading. But if you can create the aura of legitimacy around key items in your negotiation, it can work to your advantage.

An unusual but illustrative use of the aura of legitimacy was related to me by a young salesman who was hired by a builder to show a model home to be built on several nearby acres of land. The salesman went to the model home early in the morning of the day the advertised showing was to take place. While inspecting the home, he noticed about a foot of water in the basement—and prospective buyers are on their way. "Wow, what did you do?" I asked. He replied, "I got a yardstick, dipped it into the water and made a chalk line to mark the water level. Then I put the yardstick near the basement staircase." Now I was intrigued, so I asked, "What did you do when a prospect came into the house?" He smiled and said, "When they looked into the basement they were shocked to see that foot of water and asked me about it. I told them the builder wanted to prove that the basement was watertight so he filled it with water. I then picked up the yardstick, put it in the water and showed them that the level of the water matched the chalk mark." "See," I told them, "Not one drop has leaked out!" Now what he did may certainly be considered unethical and I don't recommend it, but who among us would not be convinced by the aura of legitimacy the salesman's fertile mind created. I wouldn't have questioned it, and neither did any of the prospective buyers. Before you judge the salesman too harshly I must tell you that immediately after the "open house" ended the salesman brought the leaky basement problem to the attention of the builder. The builder, who was reputable, was very upset and called in a professional to assess the problem. The professional dug a hole in the basement and learned that the model home straddled an underground stream which had been swollen by an unusual amount of rain. A sump pump was installed in the model house and all other houses in the tract of land to cure the problem if it arose in the future. As a result of the salesman's actions the homebuyers got an even better house.

I suggest that you use the aura of legitimacy whenever you can ethically do so, and don't be fooled by the other side's attempts to use it.

Aiming High and Holding Back Gets Results

Learn to hold back. No one should present his or her best offer too early, or give up too many concessions early in the game. To get the best possible deal, you need to master patience and strategic thinking.

For example, let's say you're in the furniture store and you find the perfect living room set, it's priced at $4,000 which you think is a fair price that you might be willing to pay. It is a mistake to convey any of your feelings to the salesperson. If you tell her this, you've lost the negotiation. You might win little concessions but a major one is an impossibility.

Instead, you might tell the salesperson, "This living room set is priced way too high and it's not quite what I had in mind. Maybe I would consider it if the price were right."

This message starts a far different line of negotiation. She asks you, "How much would you be willing to pay for it?" You say, "About $2,000." She counters with, "I couldn't possibly sell it for a price so low, but how about $3,600?" Now one of your good negotiating techniques locks in and you come back with, "That's a start but you've got to do better."

Through this process, you might ultimately get the price down to one you can live with. When you do, tell the salesperson, "You drive a very hard bargain. It's much more than I wanted to spend but I'll take it." This will create a feeling of satisfaction in the salesperson's mind—a necessary element in every negotiation.

People Have an Innate Fear of Superiority in Others

Human nature inhibits us in many ways. For example, people have an innate fear of going into a situation in which they believe that the other side has more money or more power or expertise. People believe they won't be able to hold their own with an "old master" or someone more experienced, more powerful, more forceful. If you are feeling intimidated by someone you need to negotiate with, try to overcome that feeling and relate to the person one-on-one. The key is to get to him on a human level and establish rapport. If he uses four-letter words, perhaps you can find common ground by using similar language. If he is sophisticated and intellectual, you need to match that style.

From the other side, people are equally uncomfortable if they think you are superior. People usually prefer dealing with equals, so if you give someone an opening and make him feel like an equal, you will go a long way toward undoing the problem.

Dumb Is Smart

Remember, things are not always what they seem. People might play dumb to gain more from you and, as always, two can play that game.

We tend, for example, to assume that we have to simplify explanations for someone with a heavy foreign accent. That is often not the case. Some people use their accent to gain a tremendous advantage in negotiation, and it works. Do not talk down to other people, and certainly do not give out more information than you intend to.

From the other side, you too can be smart by playing dumb. We've all had the experience of having someone condescend to us, and it makes us mad. But instead of showing it, we let her continue with the explanation. Look perplexed. Let her think you're dumb and you might just pick up a lot of information without having to say anything. At times, just sitting and listening is the smart move. The less talking you do, and the more talking the other side does, the smarter you become. One of the best examples of the effective use of the "dumb is smart" concept was effectively utilized by Sol Goldman, a New York real estate mogul with a plain peasant look that concealed a razor-sharp negotiating mind. He and I were in a seller's office seeking to buy an office building for $15 million all cash, which Sol thought would be a fair price to pay. Sol asked the seller, "How much do you want for the building?" The seller replied, "$15 million all cash." Goldman raised his voice to a little below a shout and said, "What?" He sounded as if he couldn't understand how the price was so high. The seller took one look at Sol's pained expression and said, "Well, maybe that price is a little too high, I would consider $14 million all cash." Once again, but in an even louder voice Goldman said, "What?" The seller thought he was antagonizing Sol and said, "I would consider taking a few million dollars cash off the price by taking back a mortgage with 6 percent interest." For the third time, Goldman said, "What?" The seller relented again and said, "If you're really interested in buying the building, I might even do better on the mortgage terms." I marveled at Goldman's negotiating technique. He was willing to buy the building for $15 million all cash, which was the seller's initial demand. But after just three "Whats" he already had a $1 million price reduction and an offer of financing terms that was subject to further negotiation. Dumb was smart!

OPERATE ON ZIFF'S PRINCIPLE OF LEAST EFFORT

Don't overlook the important negotiating tool I mentioned in an earlier chapter. People will put in the least amount of effort to accomplish the goal. They will not do more work or research than they feel is absolutely necessary. This finding came from Ziff's intensive study into how people act. Now that you know this, it should become clear that if you expend as much time and effort as possible, you will usually win every major point in the negotiation. The same principle applies to all documents. Whoever has control of the written documents also has control of the negotiation. When you prepare the documents, the other side never knows what you left out or added, but you do. The readers usually concentrate on what they read. For them to find the voids and fill them in requires a lot of thought, time, and effort. The results of Ziff's experiments indicates that there is a good likelihood they will never do it.

Everybody Loves a Freebie

Every good salesperson knows that giving away something for free often clinches the deal. If you watch the successful infomercials on television you will see what I mean. "Buy two and get one free" is often their spiel. People who fall for it will then own three items they didn't really want—but they just couldn't pass up a deal. There is always something a smart negotiator can throw in as a sweetener. "No payments for two years," "a one-year warranty instead of the usual 90-day one," "a free tank of gasoline," and so on. A house builder in a difficult negotiation for a $400,000 house might win the day by saying to a prospective buyer, "If you sign today, I'll throw in a state of the art GE microwave oven." At a cost $200 or $300 at the most, the deal goes through. If the builder offered to reduce the price of the house by that same amount, it probably wouldn't achieve the same result. It may be a small thing, but if it's a free—that's what people will remember. The dollar amount doesn't really matter. The allure of getting something free is so powerful that people often overlook the more important issues.

People Believe That One Good Turn Deserves Another

The idea of "one good turn deserves another" is imbedded in our culture and can be used as an effective tool at an appropriate time in the negotiation. The concept is entirely different from a "freebie"; it's an exchange along the lines of, "If I do something for you, such as conceding a negotiation point, then you have to do something for me." To use this technique effectively, make a list of all the open issues before yielding on any of them. Don't enlighten the other side as to which of the issues are important to you and which are not. After you've listed them all, say to your adversary, "If we agree on all these items, do we have a deal?"

If the answer is "no"; keeping listing issues until you get a "yes." As you listen to all the open items, mentally prioritize them in order of importance. Start with the items that are of the least importance to you. You should vigorously negotiate each point and finally yield on them reluctantly. Intersperse the major items and fight for them as well. The difference between a good negotiator and a poor negotiator is that the good negotiator exchanges minor losses for major wins. The "one good turn" theory makes the other side willing to exchange, but the exchange does not have to involve items of equal value nor does it have to be one for one. Surrendering five items you don't really need to get the one you really want makes the negotiation easier. Simply say, "I gave in on the last five items, now be fair and give me this one." This technique only works if you cloak the minor items you will give up with an equal or greater value than the major items you want to win. If you do that, the results will be impressive.

Invoke the Power of the Simple Solution

Everyone finds it easy to succumb to the attraction of a simple solution, but you should be careful in determining how and when to use this principle. Suggest a simple solution only when it's to your advantage. Here are four examples of statements that can lend themselves to simple solutions:

1. *"Let's split the difference."* You will want to offer this simple solution only when such a split is to your advantage. For example, you're arguing with someone about price. You want to pay

94

$20,000 for an item and the seller is asking $30,000. You're actually willing to pay $25,000, but you don't reveal that. When the negotiation gets to a point the seller indicates he will accept $26,000, you can say, "Look I want to pay $20,000 and you're now asking $26,000. I tell you what, let's split the difference." There is an excellent chance that the deal will close at $23,000 because it has the appearance of being fair to both sides.

2. *"Let's discuss this later."* At some time in a negotiation, heated arguments occur, tempers may flare, and both sides dig in and won't budge. Does that mean it can't be resolved? No. Does it mean that you shouldn't push to resolve it now? Yes. You should calmly propose putting it aside for now and tackling other things, which are less controversial. Hopefully, when "later" arrives more issues will have been resolved between the parties, more "invested time" will have been spent, and the environment will be more conducive to reaching an amicable settlement.

3. *"Let's let somebody else decide."* This is a simple solution because it removes the decision from all parties on the firing line and lets both sides off the hook temporarily. For example, when a thorny issue cannot be resolved between you and your adversary, you can say, "Why don't you take it back to your boss and let him decide this issue?" This tactic gives your adversary the opportunity to get someone else on his team who was not privy to everything that took place in the negotiations to be involved in the decision-making process. I am not saying that you must accept the decision of the additional party as an arbitrator but that decision may be rejected in whole or in part and now the negotiations have a new starting point.

4. *"Let's think outside the box."* This idea—creative solutions to tough problems—is often a welcome suggestion. No one enjoys a deadlock so if you propose something creative, it is likely to get a positive response from the other side.

Most People Refuse to Recognize or Correct Their Own Shortcomings

This is a crucial flaw in human behavior. Most people have weak spots in their abilities. Some people are terrible with figures. If you are such a person, take along a calculator or bring an accountant into your negotiations. This will cover that area of weakness. Others have trouble quickly reading and understanding documents. If this is you, don't even think of reading any complex document in five minutes under pressure. You'd be better off to say, "I have to get my lawyer to review this and I'll get back to you." That kind of self-preservation doesn't usually happen. People hate to appear inadequate and will suffer through their inadequacies and try to hide them because they don't want to admit they are bad at something. They don't want to show their deficiencies to the other side. You can use their shortcomings to your advantage by exploiting them whenever possible. There is nothing illegal or immoral in doing that, if they are willing to negotiate as if they had no shortcomings or deficiencies, that's their decision and you should accept it.

People Appreciate Others Who Can Admit Their Mistakes

It is very disarming to simply say, "I made a mistake." For example, I'm a building contractor and I say I will do the renovations you want for a total price of $120,000. When I send you the written contract, I insert a price of $140,000 You are going to be upset when you see the higher price. Your initial reaction is to say, "We agree on a price and now you're raising it?" The way to stop further animosity is to say, "I made an honest mistake. I didn't take into account the fact that the price of marble and other materials needed are much higher now."

What can you say? It stops the discussion cold. When somebody you trusted admits he made a mistake, it is perceived as an indication of strength of character and the human tendency is to forgive. You don't want to take advantage of someone who admits a mistake. For example, in a corporate setting, what do you say when someone changes the terms of a deal and tells you, "I goofed. If you insist on holding me to it, it could cost me my job!" Most people will more easily accept a change when the other person readily admits an error. Properly utilized, admitting a mistake can be a powerful negotiating tool.

Most People Are Stricken by the Deadline Syndrome

We all tend to live by deadlines. There is a time to get up so that you can get to work by a certain time. April 15 is the deadline for filing tax returns and millions of people file their returns on that specific date. Some deadlines are very important, others are not. The tendency is to believe that you *must* make a decision by every deadline, and failing to do so is tantamount to disaster.

A smart negotiator determines how important the deadline is to any negotiation. For example, in the eyes of the party facing the deadline, it is a make-or-break deal. I might tell you, "We have to make this deal now because I have a plane at 3:30. I'm out of here at 2:15."

You might tend to agree to something you might not ordinarily give up because you have my deadline in mind, and that puts you at a serious disadvantage. In reality I have no plane to catch, but I'm putting pressure on you to act quickly. My plan is to delay making any deal until the last possible moment and force you to finalize things and permit me to catch my plane.

The person who believes he *must* meet a deadline is at a clear disadvantage—especially if the other side is aware of the deadline.

People Practice the "Invested Time" Philosophy

Anyone who has worked on a transaction for an extended period of time is certainly psychologically and maybe monetarily "invested" because of the amount of time and money that has been spent in attempting to complete a transaction. Not closing the deal means that time and money is lost forever. If the time invested by the parties is disproportionate, the side with the least time invested has an advantage because it costs them less if the deal aborts. A good strategy for you to employ is to get the other side to invest as much time and money in the deal as possible while minimizing your expenditure. When the deal is in jeopardy, people will often seek to close the deal to justify the time and money already spent.

People Tend to Dwell on Their Own Power Limits

People are aware of their own constrictions. The most common of these is time. People are continuously monitoring and judging themselves, often far more harshly than anyone else does. The idea that "time is money" relates back to the invested time principle, but it also is felt as a power limit by people if they don't have the necessary time to spend to negotiate effectively. Another power limit is the ability to commit the amount of money necessary to do the deal. If you're concerned about your limited ability to pay for something, this will hamper how you negotiate. If your boss gave you the authority to buy the building for $500,000 then when the price nears or exceeds $500,000 your negotiation tactics will change drastically. Try to learn the limitations that govern your counterpart in any negotiation and use that knowledge to formulate your strategy.

Before we leave the subject of the psychology of negotiating, I want to make you aware that several tactics can be used concurrently in any phase of a negotiation.

For example, assume I am a car manufacturer and I want to entice John Q. Public to buy my vehicles. Following Ziff's principle of least resistance I will give you a lot of information that you need to know in order to make a favorable decision. I would give you the sale price, gas mileage, horsepower, and standard and optional features (the aura of legitimacy) of comparable vehicles of other manufacturers that show my cars in the most favorable light. I would offer a "Donald Trump" limited edition of 5,000 cars (people want what others want or cannot have) to anyone who orders one within 30 days (the deadline syndrome). Each owner would receive a special plaque (everyone loves a "freebie") with Donald Trump's signature certifying the authenticity of the limited edition. Used in combination, its very likely that these psychological negotiation principles would make most people willing to pay a much higher price than without them. Find your own creative ways to combine these tactics when you're negotiating your next deal.

7

INFORMATION IS POWER

Become the *Expert on the Topic*
You're Negotiating

ILEARNED MANY years ago that information you've gathered from *outside* the negotiation dialogue gives you a tremendous advantage. If you know something the other side doesn't, or, better yet, if you have information they didn't want you to know, it changes the whole picture.

Many years ago in the 1960s, I represented two of New York's biggest real estate investors, Sol Goldman and Alex DiLorenzo Jr. In late September, they had purchased from William Zeckendorf Sr. an operating lease covering the Graybar Building—a large 30-story office building across from Grand Central Terminal. Bill Zeckendorf was the head of Webb & Knapp—a public company that was a major developer and owner of extensive and diverse real estate interests. My clients purchased the operating lease for $4 million and physically took over the operation of the building; but, the whole transaction should have been approved in advance by the life insurance company that owned the ground lease on the property. Zeckendorf assigned us the operating lease without the insurance company's consent but said, "Don't worry, I will get the consent. If for any reason I don't get it by December 31, I'll repay the $4 million plus a $400,000 penalty." I made sure that the contract of sale contained that provision. Since Webb & Knapp was a substantial public company and Zeckendorf had a reputation for integrity, we accepted the assignment of lease and paid Zeckendorf $4 million. We had no doubt that he would obtain the necessary consent since the penalty was so high.

Throughout my negotiations with Zeckendorf, he told me getting the consent was a mere formality and it was not going to be a problem. I continually pestered him about the consent and his standard answer was, "George, the landlord is a huge insurance company, and I have a great working relationship with the decision makers, but it takes them time to complete the paperwork." I accepted this for a while, but then began to wonder, "It's only a simple consent that's required, it shouldn't take this long." On November 15, only 45 days before the December 31 deadline, I became suspicious. I felt something was very wrong. So, even though Zeckendorf had specifically told me not to do so, I called the insurance company's representative directly, introduced myself as Goldman's attorney and inquired about the status of the consent. I was told that on September 15 the bank had sent Zeckendorf a letter stating that it would not grant consent, and that unless our operating lease was reassigned back to Zeckendorf by December 31, it was going to claim a default and seek to terminate the lease entirely.

That bit of knowledge gave me tremendous power and guidance in how to deal with Zeckendorf from that time on. Now I knew that everything Zeckendorf had told us was false and that the deal was in jeopardy. More important was the knowledge that he was intentionally hiding a very important fact from me and from my clients. It was obvious that he could no longer be trusted. I immediately created a new negotiating environment centered on terminating the deal and getting the $4.4 million Zeckendorf had agreed to pay. When I told Sol Goldman what I had learned, he called Zeckendorf and promptly called for a meeting in Zeckendorf's office. At the meeting, Goldman demanded immediate repayment of the $4 million he had invested. Zeckendorf said, "Sol, I admit I owe you the money but I don't have $4 million." Zeckendorf figured Goldman would come up with a compromise. He was dead wrong. In a quiet voice, Goldman said, "Bill, as much as I hate to do so I can afford to lose the $4 million. But you know the TV program that starts—'News was made this day?' Well, tonight there will be an announcement on television that Webb & Knapp is facing a charge of criminal fraud. If we don't settle this, I'm going right from here to the district attorney. I'm going to flush your company down the drain, and your stock will be worthless. You won't be able to take advantage of someone else." Bill Zeckendorf took one look at Sol Goldman's expression and turned to me and said, "George, I've finally met my match, but I've got an idea. Sol, would you take my leasehold interest in the Chrysler Building in exchange for the interest in the Graybar?" Sol replied, "Sure, if the numbers work." The next day I had a contract covering the exchange. One of the provisions indicated that Zeckendorf couldn't assign his interest in the Chrysler lease without the consent of Lazard Freres Co. I asked Zeckendorf, "What happens if you don't get that consent quickly?" Zeckendorf replied, "I'll give Sol another $250,000." Recognizing this as a viable alternative, Goldman agreed to the revision. Guess what, Zeckendorf didn't get that consent either.

Since Goldman and DiLorenzo had taken over operation of the Graybar Building, I had made a few leases at high rents that increased the value of the building. Knowing that, Zeckendorf proceeded to make a deal to sell the Graybar lease to another developer for a higher price. He told Goldman that he would pay him all that he owed by noon on December 31, but if he did so he wanted Goldman to waive the $250,000 penalty for the Chrysler Building fiasco. Goldman agreed, and I was told everything was set to close by noon on December 31. I went to Zeckendorf's office at 10 A.M. on that day with the understanding that I would deliver the assignment of lease for the Graybar Building, in exchange for a certified check for $4.4 million plus the other agreed-on adjustments. December 31 was a Friday. The banks closed at 3:00 P.M., and since nothing had happened by that time, I asked one of Zeckendorf's lawyers to show me the certified check. I was told, "Oh, we have a bank officer here and he will certify any checks we need regardless of the hour." My anxiety was growing by the minute, so I called Sol Goldman and told him what was happening. He told me to get the check for the

$250,000 due from the Chrysler deal immediately or leave. I told Zeckendorf this, and in 10 minutes, I had the $250,000 check in my hands.

I called Goldman again, and he said, "Give Zeckendorf until midnight to hand you a certified check for the full amount we claim, in which event you can give him his $250,000 check back. But if he doesn't deliver, I want you to leave." In my few years of experience, I had never faced such a pressure situation with millions riding on the outcome. One thing I knew for certain was that I would not trust Zeckendorf or any of his associates.

Since it was New Year's Eve, at 6:00 P.M., I asked an associate of mine, Ed Spivack, to take my place at the closing. I told him I was going to a party, but if he needed me he could call me. I told him that the original assignment of lease was in the briefcase on the table. (He didn't know that I had it in my pocket—that's how much I trusted the other side.) I laid out three inflexible guidelines for him to follow: (1) He was to exchange the lease assignment only after he received a certified check for $4.4 million, plus the agreed amount of the adjustments; (2) He was not to eat any food or drink any liquid that didn't come out of a sealed container that he opened himself; and (3) If he didn't have the appropriate check by the stroke of midnight he was to leave immediately.

The rest of this saga was told to me by Ed Spivack. He said that at various times he was shown certified checks, but never one for the right amount. At 11:45 P.M., he was told to go upstairs and they would show him the check for the right amount. Ed went upstairs and was told the check wasn't ready yet and he should go back downstairs and they would bring the check to him. When he returned to the office he had been in on the floor below, he noticed the briefcase had been moved. He looked inside and learned that the assignment of lease was missing. He was terrified and immediately called me and said, "They went through my briefcase and took the assignment while I was upstairs!" I told him to calm down and explained that since I didn't trust them, I had taken the original with me. I told him that if it were needed, I'd leave the party and bring it in. Someone in Zeckendorf's employ was listening in on this conversation and took immediate action in an attempt to place Goldman in default. They kept delivering seemingly certified checks in various amounts, but never the right amount. Finally, at 12:01 A.M., they tried to give Ed a check for the right amount and demanded that he deliver the assignment of lease. He told them his authority to accept the check ceased at midnight and he was leaving. Ed headed for the elevators and when it arrived one of Zeckendorf's associates told the elevator operator, "If you take this guy down you're fired!" Since they wouldn't let him use the elevator he walked down 13 flights of stairs to get out of the building. The next day Zeckendorf called me and said, "George, Sol is in big trouble." I replied, "Bill, we're still holding the lease, so we'll do what is necessary to make peace with the insurance company and we'll bring a lawsuit against you that will wipe you out." He said, "Meet me at my house in Connecticut, and I'll solve everything."

I did, and he did. On January 5, I delivered the assignment of lease and got paid in full. I am telling you this story to show you the lengths that so-called reputable people will go when there's a great deal of money at stake. This story also illustrates how knowledge is power in a negotiation: Obtaining critical information the other side doesn't want you to have helps clarify the real issues and dictates your course of conduct. Once you find out that someone on the other side has lied to you or failed to reveal a material fact, you can never resurrect the trust you had in that person, and you should use every means at your disposal to protect yourself.

There are two kinds of knowledge in a negotiation that are both powerful, but slightly different: actual knowledge and apparent knowledge.

ACTUAL KNOWLEDGE

Obviously, the more knowledge you possess, the better you are going to fare during a negotiation. The person who walks in with well-organized research and facts to back up his position is invariably going to outperform the other side. The person who has learned as much as possible about the people he's talking to is well ahead of the game. He knows their strengths and weaknesses, even their hobbies, education, and career path. Everything you pick up along the way about the other side, no matter how seemingly insignificant it seems, is valuable.

Actual knowledge can be dangerous if it turns out to be invalid or inaccurate. Let's say you're trying to sell a home near Seattle. You gather statistics on average numbers, and you conclude, "home sales in Seattle are way down." That does not mean they will be down for your particular house or up for your town or neighborhood. You're dealing with averages here, so it won't always apply exactly to your property. It would be a mistake to negotiate on the premise that the market for your particular home is also way down. The statistics have to fit the details of your circumstance. If you're trying to sell one property in a particular area, these citywide averages are probably meaningless, although you might think they constitute actual knowledge.

Any statistical information you use is going to be reliable and accurate in varying degrees based on the circumstances: the sample, the size of the sample, and how objectively the research was conducted. Be cautious when you adopt information that you are willing to classify as actual knowledge.

You can obtain knowledge from a number of sources rather than by performing your own research. For example:

- *Use your own experience and education.* Remember one important key point. When others express opinions about the marketplace, those opinions are *always* based on averages. So, it would be hazardous for you to use averages in a negotiation when the deal concerns a specific property, rather than working with the broad market.

If you are knowledgeable, then feel free to rely on your own experience. When you don't have the experience or education you need in a given situation, then you should obtain it elsewhere. Use the Internet. Talk to as many people as you can to get advice and facts, but learn to gather valid information to supplement what you already know.

- *Discuss relevant issues with outside professionals.* It's unavoidable that you're going to go up against issues beyond your own expertise. You need to consult with outside experts when this occurs. This happens all the time in negotiations. People confer with their accountant, attorney, financial advisor, or when needed, someone who is highly specialized. Even attorneys specialize in narrow fields, so when an issue comes up beyond their expertise, they talk with other attorneys. Even though I consider myself an expert in real estate law, I have no hesitation in calling another attorney in the field when I'm faced with a situation I have never seen before. If I'm not bashful you shouldn't be either. Always be on the lookout for a good specialist who can help you.

- *Hold discussions with all the necessary parties on your side.* Most people operate under the restrictions placed on them by an organization, a spouse, or a budget. We all know about these constraints. However, you should never overlook the contribution that any number of other people can make to build your knowledge base. The use of other resources isn't limited to the chain of command or getting budget approval. It can be a simple matter of channeling in to someone else's knowledge to enhance your own.

You also need to be aware that when negotiations fail, it is usually caused by people on *your* side, not the other side. It's important to have discussions beforehand to ensure that you are aware of all points of view. This makes you a more effective negotiator.

APPARENT KNOWLEDGE

The second kind of knowledge—apparent knowledge—is perhaps a little more subtle, but equally important in negotiation.

If the other side *believes* that you are very knowledgeable about a subject, by reputation or even by your use of buzz words, then they might come to the conclusion that you really know what you are talking about. As a result, they might be less inclined to try certain tactics because they feel they wouldn't work with you.

This *apparent knowledge*—whether based on reality or only on perception—wins you some points because the other side's assumptions take over. They treat you with more respect. If I go into a meeting, and the topic of lease options comes up, I might say, "I haven't dealt with options that much, so I'll have to look into it." The other side will immediately believe that they have the advantage, especially if they are knowledgeable in that area. But if I say, "Yes, I've handled dozens of lease options and, in fact, I began my career working with a talented real estate investor who virtually invented lease options," then the other side will have a completely different picture.

The interesting thing about this is that virtually no one would challenge my claim to expertise. The truth might be that I have very little actual knowledge in this area, but it is unlikely that people will respond by asking me, "Who was that client?" or "Exactly how many lease options have you negotiated?" Instead, the presumption of my expertise is established by my staking a claim, and that will rarely be challenged.

With this in mind, try to be confident when you walk into a meeting and begin negotiating; that is often all it takes. This is one of the ironies of human nature. People are inclined to give you the benefit of the doubt until they have compelling proof to contradict that belief. If you claim to be an expert, the other side is probably going to believe you. Apparent knowledge can sometimes be more powerful than actual knowledge, but be aware that if the other side probes your apparent knowledge too deeply, you may lose your credibility.

There are two things to remember about apparent knowledge and how you can utilize it as a tool in negotiation:

1. *You don't have to be an expert on the topic of the negotiation to look like one, especially if you recognize a pattern emerging.* If you are familiar with a specific personality type or a ploy the other side is using, that can be more valuable than actual knowledge. If you have previously dealt with General Motors, you are better equipped to negotiate with Ford Motor Company. You already understand the philosophy. There will be a similar mentality. A corporation in the same business deals with the same competitive and market forces. So you, as a negotiator, are able to use these experiences—based on the general information you hold—to communicate with the other side in a way that counts.

   Sometimes, people with incredible amounts of actual knowledge are virtually useless when the negotiation becomes critical. They might be so focused on facts and data that they fail to appreciate the ploys the other side is using. They have a blind spot. They are knowledgeable about the topic, but their negotiating experience is lacking. Once again, actual knowledge can be less important than apparent knowledge.

2. *In a negotiation, you are likely to draw on your experience in comparable situations—but this situation may be different in important ways.* No two groups of people are going to be identical, and neither will everyone react to the same circumstances in the same way.

If I have negotiated 15 deals with real estate developers over the past year, and you're number 16, I am naturally going to start out assuming that you are going to act and react in much the same way as the previous 15 developers.

I say to myself, "This tactic worked before under similar circumstances with a different adversary, let's see if it works now." But what if the situation is not identical? There are usually a large number of variables, and all of these are going to affect how people act and react.

You may have greater insight about the topic than the other 15 developers, or you might have keener instincts about negotiating with me. I assume the general information you possess is equal to that of the other 15 developers, but I keep an open mind and I watch how the discussion unfolds. All of the other developers focused almost exclusively on the bottom line. "How much money am I going to make?" was continually on their minds, but you seem to be more concerned with the aesthetic quality of a development. You want to design and build exceptional projects. This tells me a great deal about how I need to alter my style. In all of the previous negotiations, the developers didn't care where the land was situated. They only wanted the cheapest land they could find, to create the fastest construction schedule, to maximize their turnover, and to walk away with their profits, never looking back. Understanding this, my negotiation strategy with them focused on the dollars and cents. I knew this was the focus of the other side, and so I was able to get concessions of other kinds as long as I could convince the developers that they would make a great deal of money.

Clearly, in negotiating with you, I am going to have to convince you that the site is *suitable* for what you have in mind; that it is harmonious with surrounding land use; and that air quality, noise, and other environmental issues are going to be acceptable. If I ignore these factors, I will not be able to negotiate with you successfully. I have to change my style to suit your needs, and I need to understand what makes you tick if I expect to succeed in our negotiation.

In this kind of a situation, I begin with general information about "how developers think" about their projects. But in fact, I now learn that not all developers approach projects in the same way. You are not focused on the bottom line, which at first perplexes me because I expected you to be like everyone else. Toward the end of the negotiation, I might even ask, "Why is your focus on design and aesthetics, instead of profit?" You might reply, "I have discovered that investing more money in the quality of a project is more satisfying and ironically, more profitable as well."

This expands my insight into developers in general. Now I have increased my own general knowledge of that industry. That observation—that design is sometimes more of a driving force than profits—is only part of the picture. The outcome is also enlightening because it changes my perspective (increasing my general knowledge). You are also interested in profits, but you approach the issue by combining profits with quality work.

Donald Trump is a perfect example of this philosophy. Anyone who has seen Trump Tower on 5th Avenue, recognizes that he refused to cut corners. The overall impression, from the ground floor up, is that the whole building is high quality. Trump personally played a direct role in the design, because he knew that value would ultimately depend on it. Anything with the Trump name on it had to be luxurious. Trump Tower was lavish in design, but an extremely profitable investment.

This is the kind of insight you gain by expanding your apparent knowledge. You want to be *the* expert on the topic under negotiation, but you can gain that knowledge in many different ways. Actual and apparent knowledge add up to amazing insights, even when you are negotiating with someone on a topic you've dealt with many, many times. If you listen well and are open-minded in your discussions with the person on the other side, you will broaden your knowledge. Everyone can learn something from everyone else, and you will definitely be smarter going into your next negotiation and those that follow.

8

Keep Multiple Solutions in Mind

Remain Flexible and Creative about What You Need and Want

You always have negotiating power if you can force yourself to *walk away* from a deal, either temporarily or permanently. This doesn't mean that walking away permanently is a good idea unless the transaction has reached the hopeless stage. If it's hopeless, give it up and go on to something else. But a disagreement or deadlock is also an opportunity to craft a different deal, perhaps even a better deal for both sides. This applies in every negotiation. The more open-minded you remain, the better you will fare when disagreements arise.

I saw a good example of this principle when Donald Trump was negotiating a licensing deal with Macy's for the "Donald J. Trump Signature Collection" of men's clothing. Macy's through its affiliate, Federated, is the country's biggest retailer that caters to customers who are likely buyers of the Donald J. Trump Signature Collection. Trump wanted to persuade Macy's into taking the line, while keeping open the possibility of also marketing it elsewhere, Macy's wanted an exclusive so that it would be the only retail chain handling the Donald J. Trump Signature Collection. Because Macy's is such a big retailer, it felt it could dictate terms and it wanted the exclusive without any conditions.

Ordinarily, someone who wants to market a product wants mass distribution and does not like to have that product limited to any one retailer. Our premise initially was that we weren't going to give anyone an exclusive. When Macy's insisted on an exclusive arrangement, and we wanted Macy's buying power, we were forced to change the premise. But our position was that in exchange for an exclusive, Macy's would have to satisfy certain conditions, such as placing the merchandise in a minimum number of stores, guaranteeing an advertising budget, and setting aside a minimum amount of display space in each store. How big the space was going to be and where it would be located in each store was a subject of much discussion. We wanted a minimum commitment as to how much store space, time, and effort Macy's was going to spend promoting the line. Macy's balked at the concept claiming that it was the expert in merchandising and we should rely on it in that regard rather than dictate terms. The extent of Macy's commitment was a major stumbling block. Ultimately, Trump came to the conclusion that sometimes you have to go with your gut feeling in a transaction. After speaking to the head of the merchandising division and the CEO of Macy's, he felt certain they would maximize the opportunity, and he gave up most of his merchandising control rights.

Both sides came out of the deal satisfied that they got what they could live with, even though the basic premise each had started with had changed. Trump was flexible enough to recognize that granting an exclusive could give him the power to get something else he didn't have before. The Macy's executives recognized the potential value of an exclusive on the Donald J. Trump Signature Collection and made concessions they never made before.

In any negotiation, it is likely that some type of stumbling block will arise. Someone may draw a line in the sand and take the position, "It's got to be this way, or there's no deal."

If that happens, your task will be to find something that each side can live with, to make the deal more flexible, and to propose alternatives. So for example, if they tell you that they have to get $100,000 for a piece of equipment and there's no getting around it, what can you say? Perhaps you would be willing to agree to the amount, but negotiate extended payment terms. What happens if you offer to pay them $20,000 over five years? Unless they absolutely have to get all the money right now—an unusual situation—there is likely to be some room for negotiation. Maybe you can discuss an interest rate. Or maybe they would agree to reduce the price in exchange for a share of the future profits you will receive from the use of the equipment, or for an option on another property you own, or some other novel arrangement. Maybe that demand for $100,000 *cash* isn't cast in stone. But neither side can find out, unless each is willing to discuss it.

This is why a good negotiator hesitates before making irrefutable statements. If they tell you they *must* have $100,000 right now, and you only want to pay them $80,000, the parties can lock horns all day, but nothing will get resolved until one of them proposes an alternative solution. Your adversary might say, "I want the $100,000, but I don't actually need all of it at the moment. I do need it within three years."

Now we're talking. There is a basis for more discussion. So, perhaps you could come back and ask them, "Why three years? If you run it out over five years, you make more interest, and the loan is still secured. I'll give you a valid lien on the equipment if you want it; it will minimize your risk."

If at any time during the discussion you sense that your adversary is closing his mind—interrupting, losing patience, raising his voice—you should try to calm him down. Your objective is to send out a flexibility message and to invite him to hear what you have to say, and perhaps respond in kind.

Rather than letting the noise level escalate, you could respond to the increase in the volume of your adversary's voice by lowering the volume of yours, which will cause him to listen more intently. It might be effective if you quietly say, "Just hear me out, I think you're going to like my idea."

If you can get him to listen to you, both sides can win. As long as the dialogue continues, it demonstrates that both sides are practicing flexibility. This is how some tough negotiations turn into satisfying ones.

If the two sides can't get over a sticking point, you might suggest bringing in a third party to mediate. It sometimes takes a neutral third party to get through these tough areas—and often, their solutions are so obvious and so simple, both sides are amazed that they didn't think of it themselves. It is often a matter of egos getting in the way, or of one or both sides being overly committed to their version of how things should turn out.

Flexibility has several different aspects worthy of some discussion. Three come to mind: Defining the bottom line, different kinds of flexibility, and the apparent versus the real bottom line. You may have noticed that I often suggest many different things you might do. As I said in the beginning of this book, the frustrating and fascinating thing about negotiation is that there *never* is a right or wrong way to proceed. A negotiating problem is not like a disease that can be cured by a dose of some known medication. There is a huge amount of trial and error throughout any complex negotiation. If something isn't working, try something else until you achieve the response you seek. If after reading this book, you think that you now have all the answers for any negotiation situation, think again. However, if you follow my guidelines, each negotiation will be a valuable learning experience, and one day you will come to the realization that you're one hell of a negotiator.

DEFINE THE BOTTOM LINE IN ITS VARIOUS ASPECTS

The *bottom line* is most often thought of in financial terms. It can also be defined by understanding the trade-off value of long-term control for some immediate concessions of equivalent value. Most people focus on a purely financial outcome—how much do you get or how much is it going to cost? This can be very shortsighted.

As a starting point, I want to talk about the financial bottom line because it's usually at the heart of the majority of deals you will negotiate.

Review the Financial Bottom Line in All of Its Aspects

There is more to the financial bottom line than the price one side pays to the other, usually much more. You have to think about not only the price, but often financing and payment terms, imposed conditions, and the interaction between how much you pay for what you get. This may be the crux of the negotiation, and the one part where it is most difficult to achieve an acceptable compromise.

The bottom line caveat may be applied in many ways. For example, most people buying real estate spend a great deal of energy arguing about the price, when they should be discussing what the deal includes. What's the condition of the roof? Are the appliances in good working order? Have there ever been any leaks in the basement? Are lighting fixtures, carpeting, and furniture included? The answers to these questions will be helpful in negotiating the price.

Use Marketing Advantages to Make the Bottom Line Better

Remember the Macy's licensing agreement? Trump did not want to give Macy's an exclusive, but by negotiating a marketing benefit to the deal, he was able to get a far better outcome than he'd originally thought—and Macy's got their exclusive.

You might be able to negotiate all kinds of extra concessions in exchange for an adjustment in the price. For example, an author is negotiating with a publisher. He wants a certain amount for an advance, but the publisher wants to pay only about half of that. Does this mean they can't do the deal? Of course not. The parties continue to negotiate. The author gets the publisher to agree to set up a specific advertising budget to promote his book, which will generate more sales and more income for both sides. The publisher agrees if the author make several public appearances to promote the book. The author walks away believing that the concessions make the deal equal to or better than what he'd been asking for; and the publisher is happy because it can pay a smaller advance, which reduces its financial risk if the book turns out to be a bomb.

Marketing is a great venue that lends itself to flexibility. In so many deals, flexibility can have a greater impact on the overall transaction than price itself. Any time you are negotiating with people who are going to market something for you, or you are going to market something for them, pay close attention to that aspect of the deal. Think about this. Isn't marketing found in every transaction? Don't you have to sell yourself, your qualifications, your enthusiasm, or the benefits of dealing with you in each deal? That's absolutely true and you must never forget it even for a moment. You are always selling throughout every phase of any negotiation.

Consider Long-Term Benefits versus Short-Term Negatives

Most people have the tendency to think short-term in their negotiations. This leads to inflexibility. For example, if you're talking to someone who just wants to get the price he wants, it may be to your long-term advantage to give up on a price reduction in exchange for something that may be of far greater value in the future, like the possibility of future dealings. Donald Trump has skillfully used ancillary benefits to make spectacular real estate deals. These included buying unused air rights from adjoining property owners at higher than normal prices so he could legally build the highest residential tower in New York City. Trump paid a very high price to Tiffany for its air rights, but as part of the deal, he got the option Tiffany had on the adjoining parcel, which later became a part of the Trump Tower deal.

Trump knows how to deal with people, figure out what they want, and then give it to them in ways that meet their needs and also satisfy his. Because most people are short-term thinkers while he is a long-term thinker, this gives him an advantage. When Trump approached the neighboring landowners in connection with his Trump World Tower and offered to buy their unused air rights for immediate cash, the owners generally said, "Sure!" They were happy to sell something they thought they would never need or use. Trump was prepared for those who stopped to think, "Why does this guy want to buy my air rights? If he wants them so badly, maybe they're worth a whole lot more." To answer their concern, he told them that if he paid anyone else a higher price per square foot for their air rights, he would agree in the contract to pay them the higher price as well. By using this simple tactic, he was able to acquire all the unused air rights from the owners of property on the block without any holdouts.

You gain much by exchanging short-term benefits (e.g., cash, or agreeing to someone's price) for one or more long-term benefits. The ability to commence future negotiations, if needed, in a friendly environment is often worth the short-term extra cost.

USE FLEXIBILITY AS A STRATEGIC TOOL

Being flexible in a negotiation is often viewed as a bad idea. Some people think that showing any willingness to consider alternatives is a sign of weakness. This is an example of a misguided but common philosophy.

Flexibility can work to your benefit. Whenever you face a conflict, proposing possible compromises or, better yet, suggesting a different way to attack the problem, shows that you are a skilled negotiator; not that you are weak. Refusing to budge from an entrenched position is one of the symptoms of a truly weak negotiator because he or she is unwilling to explore the possibility of getting an even better deal. Any negotiator who takes a position and refuses to change it just doesn't understand how to get the maximum out of any transaction.

There Are Many Nuances to Flexibility

Because you may be flexible about a small point, does not mean you are automatically a pushover for a big point. Be aware of the necessity to separate discussions that involve minor issues from those that involve major ones. A wise strategy is to be willing, throughout the course of the negotiation, to concede small points, make concessions, give in to the other side—but only on the minor discussions.

When the major points come up, it's time to ask for reciprocation. You can say, "I gave you almost everything you asked for. It's only fair that you should give me something." This tactic is very effective. You make a series of reluctant concessions on minor points, and then insist on having your turn. One good way to plan for this is to control the agenda. Draw up a list of the issues you think should be discussed, and put it in a sequence so that all of the points on which you are willing to make concessions—the minor points— come up first. You can probably get through them relatively quickly, and let the other side win most of them. Your flexibility at this phase becomes a powerful advantage when you get to the more important points.

This brings up another crucial item. Keep track of the issues and how they get resolved. A good negotiator is also a good scorekeeper. This serves two purposes. First, it gives you leverage when you get to the major items. Second, it provides you with a series of notes to verify the terms of the deal. In this way, you can document what everyone said. In an extended negotiation, you may want to write a letter or memo to send out periodically. When it comes time to draw up a contract, your carefully detailed notes help you capture all of the terms of the deal. Of course, you should volunteer to draw up the contract, because, as I said before, it's extremely beneficial to control the documents.

Flexibility-Based Strategies Work

You need to remember that negotiating specific points is only one aspect of the bigger picture. The way you get through disagreements and the course you ultimately take might have many side trips along the way. This is where you can employ a variety of effective strategies. They are designed to create the illusion that you're being flexible, when in fact they are simply a way to get to where you want to end up.

One of these strategies was discussed in the previous section—giving in and conceding on minor points. This is a smart technique for controlling the agenda and the final outcome.

The "Dead Dog on the Table" Strategy

Another strategy is to present an idea that you know will not be acceptable and fight hard for its acceptance. Create a strong point of disagreement with the other side. You posture and vigorously fight for your idea, but ultimately you agree to give in, and then you present an alternative. Your second plan is actually what you want, but the other side doesn't know that. Compared to the first idea you presented, the second plan is much more palatable, so they are more likely to embrace it with very little resistance. This idea—presenting a terrible, unacceptable proposal only to later replace it with what you really want—is sometimes called the "dead dog on the table" strategy. This strategy makes good use of the theory of relativity. Someone on the other side will say, "I only agreed to the second proposal because the first one was horrible. I'm glad that he came up with an alternative." If neither Plan A (the dead dog strategy) nor Plan B is accepted, then you abandon them both. This abandonment may then be added to the list of concessions you've already made to be used when you want to get the other side to cave in on another major point.

BOTTOM-LINE DEFINITIONS

To improve your success as a negotiator, expand your definition of the bottom line. Successful negotiators know how to set goals, define the path to attain them, and appreciate the results from reaching those goals. This has to involve much more than the numbers aspect of a deal. Donald Trump often puts this principle to work. He invariably has some kind of vision that he wants to transform into reality. When he converted the run-down, depressed Commodore Hotel into a first-class hotel, his vision had several aspects. The task was daunting, but Trump knew that a hotel like his Grand Hyatt would lead the way to a revitalized area surrounding Grand Central Terminal; thus, building his reputation. He also knew that by gaining a reputation as someone who knew how to get things done, he would be able to achieve a high profile that would open many more doors and give him access to more rewarding and impressive projects. Trump was not thinking primarily about how much money he could make on the Grand Hyatt project. Ultimately, he did make a great deal of money from it but that was an off shoot of his broader vision. He became a white knight who structured a deal to solve *everyone's* problems concerning the property. When you define what really matters to you, that also defines what really matters for others as well.

EXPLOITING SHORT-TERM FINANCIAL THINKING IN OTHERS

As I have said before, most people are determined to focus on the dollars and cents of a deal. How much will I make or how much will it cost? This is a flaw, a blind spot in most people. And you can expertly exploit this kind of short-term thinking in others by defining something you are willing to throw in.

For example, let's say that I want to buy a building from someone. I want to pay $400,000 and she is asking $500,000. Now, I know the building is probably worth close to $500,000, but I am going to come up with a novel variation of the deal to try and bring down her price. I happen to own a piece of vacant land that has been an unending monetary headache for me. Without sewage or power lines, it has no real useful purpose, so its present value is low. I paid $10,000 for it, but obtained an appraisal indicating a value of $60,000, if developed.

I would very much like to get rid of this property, and I've been thinking of selling it for whatever I can get, probably about $10,000 at the most. I'm going to bring this piece of land into the discussion. I know that if I offered to raise my offer to $410,000 the other side would not consider that to be a serious offer. Instead, I say, "Let's change this deal a bit. If you will agree to my price of $400,000, I will *give* you a great building lot that I own in a good location, which is appraised at $60,000."

Now I can argue, "Look, I came up from $400,000 more than halfway. I am now putting an offer of $460,000 on the table, plus the additional value of my piece of land in the future. I think that's a great deal for you."

This is an example of how you can exploit your opponent's short-term financial thinking. The fact that your lot isn't doing anything for you right now and you'd gladly sell it for $10,000 isn't important. It is *potentially* worth $60,000 or more in the future. That could happen next year, or it could take 10 years. This is smart negotiating because it diverts the seller's fixation on a fixed purchase price to the potential romance of owning another piece of land. Any diversion that works for you is worth exploring with the other side.

Be Aware of Your Own Bottom-Line Vision

In any negotiation, ask yourself the following questions: "Why am I negotiating? What do I need or want from this negotiation? Am I in the deal for the excitement of the process of negotiation? Am I trying to make money so I can retire at an early age? Will this deal grant me independence?" Everyone has his or her own *bottom-line vision*, and you should never assume it is the same for all people. It often is something more intangible than the actual bottom-line number. Many people like to focus on the financial bottom line because it gives them something measurable; but in fact, they might not really know their own real bottom-line vision.

For example, some people want to be respected and known as smart investors. What they really want from a deal is acknowledgment of that fact. If you can identify your opponent's bottom-line vision as a desire for recognition, you can use it during your negotiation. You might say, for example, "I am interested in this property because, like you, I think I'm a smart investor. I recognize value and foresight when I see it. When you bought this property several years ago, it was not nearly as valuable as it is today. I can see that you had the foresight to know it was going to increase in value, but I think you have overestimated the amount of that increase."

This admission does not give up anything on your part. Someone who wants to be acknowledged as a smart investor is likely to respond to this tactic positively, and the discussion starts as to what price the seller will accept and what price you are willing to pay.

It is never enough to enter a negotiation with a single objective. If you do, you will inevitably run into problems you never considered. Creative alternatives may emerge that you never imagined at the outset. But you can define your goals in terms of a *range* of outcomes that will be acceptable to you. Conversely, when in the course of the negotiation you spontaneously present creative solutions, the other side often finds them appealing; that is especially true if they don't know the solutions were carefully preconceived. It's exciting and demonstrates that you are working to help them realize their goals.

9

WIN THROUGH DISCIPLINE

*The Deal Book, We-They List,
POST Checklist, and Other
Powerful Planning Tools*

THERE IS A human tendency to enter a negotiation without a detailed plan or strategy for getting what you want. But the more prepared you are when you begin negotiations—the more information you have about the people on the other side, their background and reputation, the issues, research on the markets—the greater the advantage you have throughout the negotiation.

A good example is found in the way that Donald Trump negotiated the deal for his television show, *The Apprentice*. It was Donald's knowledge about the people involved that made him so effective. He knew one important fact: The executive producer, Mark Burnett, needed him to make the whole idea work. Burnett, who had also produced the reality show *Survivor*, had originally wanted to give *Survivor* to NBC, but NBC balked, so the show went to CBS instead. Once *Survivor* became a hit, the concept of a good reality show being able to succeed was proven. So NBC knew they should have picked up the first show. So when Burnett came up with another idea, for a show called *The Apprentice*, it was easy to pitch it to NBC. The formula was proven, not only as a good idea, but as a hit.

For Burnett to be able to sell *The Apprentice* to NBC, he needed someone like Donald Trump who would have immediate audience recognition. Understanding Burnett's need in the negotiation, Donald told Burnett, "Okay, I'll do it, but only if we're partners and I get half of everything." Burnett agreed.

Next, Burnett and Trump met with the executives at NBC and offered them the show, and the negotiations with the network began. At first, NBC wanted an exclusive for all the rights connected with the show. Burnett and Trump refused. They finally agreed to give NBC exclusive rights only in the United States. They retained the rights to the show elsewhere in the world. Since Burnett and Trump were equal partners and both were experienced negotiators and Donald had an excellent relationship with NBC executives, they were able to accomplish this. Burnett knew that NBC was envious of CBS's success with the *Survivor* and Donald knew the key people at NBC. They were prepared. They knew NBC felt it had made a big mistake when Burnett pitched them on the *Survivor,* and they would be willing to give up something valuable to get *The Apprentice.* That something was the foreign rights.

Foreign rights included not just the right to sell the show; it included ownership of the format as well as broadcast rights outside of the United States for millions of dollars. The Trump-Burnett entity was able to sell the right to use the format or concept for the show to foreign licensees who wanted to produce their own version of *The Apprentice,* but they also had to buy *The Apprentice* as it was filmed in the United States. The foreign rights market included merchandise that became available—pens, shirts, hats with "You're Fired" embroidered on the brim, and so on. The U.S. deal in connection with those incidentals is a three-way deal, 50 percent to NBC and another 50 percent split between Trump and Burnett. Outside the United States, everything belongs to Burnett and Trump.

It was a great deal for Trump because NBC had paid a huge price for the show that included the costs involved in putting the show in the can. After the show had premiered on NBC, Burnett and Trump were free to sell the finished product throughout the rest of the world, without sharing any payments with the network.

The whole deal was based on two important facts: Donald Trump knew that Mark Burnett needed him, and Burnett knew that NBC wanted a successful reality show. I imagine it would have been entirely different if *Survivor* had not already been a hit, and no one—the network, the producer, or Donald Trump—had any idea about what to expect from *The Apprentice.*

Even in a case like this, where both sides are motivated to make a deal, the negotiation is harder than most people expect and they fail to prepare for it. Good negotiators have a game plan and prepare in advance for any contingency. You need to answer questions like these in advance:

- What are you planning to say?
- How are you going to react to what the other side says?
- What will you say if the talks come to a standstill?
- What concessions are you willing and able to make?
- What do you expect from the other side?
- Who will you be negotiating with, and what motivates them?

The more you know, the more you find out ahead of time *and* during the actual negotiation, the more control you have over the eventual outcome. Control, of course, means you explore every avenue available to achieve what you want from the negotiation. It's like coming up with a script or a storyline that you think is likely to unfold. It may not unfold exactly as you thought. But if you begin with a script (which may require revisions along the way), you are organized from the outset. The power you gain by being thoroughly prepared is magnified by the extent of the other side's lack of preparation.

How to Prepare

You gain the control you need to master negotiations by being better organized than everyone else. This is not as big a challenge as you might think, considering that most people are woefully unprepared when they enter a negotiation. People tend to think of the issues in simplistic terms. They are usually focused on negotiating price and timing, and little else; but in every negotiation there is always much more. Here are a few things to keep in mind as you prepare and organize your information in advance of a negotiation.

Dig for Information about the Other Side

Going into a negotiation, you should always start by knowing who your adversaries are. What are their backgrounds? Do they have a track record, and what does that tell you? Has anybody else dealt with them whom you know, and what can they tell you? What kind of reputation do they have? Were there complaints by others who dealt with them?

Anything that will give you any insight, no matter how seemingly insignificant, into the kinds of people you're dealing with is valuable. Negotiation generally involves a discussion of the terms—price, deadline, financing, things that are or aren't included—but it really boils down to people dealing with each other. So if you know the people and their motivations, and you can rightfully assume they know little about you, then you clearly are better equipped to succeed. With greater knowledge about the other side, you're probably going to win more points.

You can find information about people from many different sources. Check with other people who know or have dealt with the opposition. Get on the phone to someone you know and ask, "What can you tell me about this guy? Can I trust him? What's the best approach I can use in negotiating with him?"

Also check the Internet, the Bar Association (if the person is a lawyer), and the Better Business Bureau to see if there is information to be obtained from those sources. Talk to other parties in the negotiation to see what they know. In some cases, you may have preliminary discussions with someone reporting to the decision maker—an accountant, lawyer, or other executive, for example—and the boss participates later to finalize the deal. Ask these people in the early phases to tell you what they know about the boss. How does he make decisions? Does he generally move fast or slow in reaching decisions? Does he have to get someone else's approval before deciding? If you phrase your questions correctly, you can get a lot of information in a friendly way, without looking like you're just being nosy.

Presentation Guidelines during Negotiations

When I go into a negotiation, I start by determining what will be required to create a positive impression on the other side and use that to persuade them to embrace my position. Any negotiation is a selling job. To get to this point, I know I'll have to put in time and effort to identify what I think will work, why I believe I'm right about my arguments, and why I believe the other side should agree with me. I have to be prepared to make the case that my ideas are fair and reasonable. If I can convince the other side it's fair and reasonable for them as well, then my negotiating discipline pays off and everyone is pleased with the result.

Documentation Is One of the Main Keys

It has always amazed me how many people come to a negotiation basically empty-handed and shoot from the hip. This is a big mistake because documents are critical to winning points within the negotiation. Remember the aura of legitimacy—the idea that something is authentic—is based largely on what people see or read. If you have blank forms and tell the other side, "This is what we normally use," your forms with all the many conditions become the "standard forms." If you draw up a summary of research you have performed (which should be skewed in your favor), it's more readily accepted and believed when it's a printed document, rather than an oral statement of facts. If you present a written proposal of the deal as you see it, you're going to win more than the other side who often comes into the room with a legal pad and a pen, nothing more.

Take any type of documentation into the meeting that will be support your arguments and the outcome you hope to achieve. For example, if I am going to buy a roomful of furniture and I go into a furniture store where I think the price is too high, I will go in with ads from other similar furniture stores selling for less. With the documentation in front of me, I can ask the seller, "Why is your price so high?" This puts the pressure on the seller to either justify that price or offer an explanation. You have the advantage immediately because in all likelihood all the other side has is a fact sheet about his product but little or nothing about comparable prices, or the advantages or disadvantages of the competition Although they may be familiar with all the facts, when you have documentation, it's much easier to defend your position.

Your Most Powerful Tool: A *Deal Book*

There are two types of deal books and each is an infallible method of filing information for immediate retrieval. The first type of *deal book* that I will call the "general ledger" is one that Donald Trump uses every day. Even though he retains a lot of information in his head, he knows he also needs to write everything down, so he will list who called him, who he called, what was discussed, and so on. He will then have one of his three secretaries transcribe pertinent information and send it to other members of the Trump Organization who have the need to know. I use a general ledger as well, to keep a daily track of my telephone calls, everything that was said, telephone numbers, and information that requires further action. It's a spiral notebook with fixed pages (loose leaf pages are not allowed). My general ledger is my working bible and never leaves its reserved location on my desk. It enables me to keep track of what I said and what the other side's response was. In this way, if they come back later and contradict what they said, I can refer back to my notes. I also keep track of what worked and what didn't work—it's an excellent memory jogger as the negotiation proceeds.

If you find it easier, your general ledger can be kept on a notepad, index cards, computer, or PDA, but it has to be associated with a filing system that enables you to get your hands on critical information as quickly as possible. For the general ledger or the deal book to be an effective tool, it must be kept up to date. Now let's look at a deal book that is tailored for a specific transaction.

The Deal Book Is a Checklist and Organizer

The key to creating a truly effective deal book is taking careful notes on everything, writing down your plans for the negotiation, telephone numbers and addresses, and every scrap of pertinent information. If you follow that rule, everything you need for this particular deal is in one place. Remember, the more complete your deal book is, the more powerful you will be as a negotiator. An example of what a deal book might look like is shown on page 137.

This example reflects a relatively simple transaction. If the deal involved several meetings, the dates, places, and participants would be listed. All open issues would be inserted in the deal book together with the anticipated solution. Any interesting new information I obtained would be noted, together with my reaction as to how it affects the deal or my negotiation technique. The deal book should also contain an agenda for each meeting and, on a larger scale, a desired agenda for the entire negotiation that may involve a series of meetings over days or weeks, and perhaps even months. The more complex the deal, the more you need an efficient and well-organized deal book.

File # 2001-102

Client:	Donald Trump
Matter:	Lease of 29th fl. 40 Wall Street
Tenant:	Jon Smith LLC
Tenant's attorney:	Jon Pappas 462 Lexington Ave. NYC 10144 Tel (212) 234-5678 Fax (212) 356-7890
Broker:	Neil Jones CBRE Tel (212) 333-3333 Fax (212) 555-5555
Address:	100 Park Ave, NYC, NY 10008
Terms of lease:	See 4/26/06 letter from broker attached

Action taken:

5/1   Prepared initial draft of lease and sent 2 copies to Pappas.

5/6   Rec'd Pappas comments. Need review.

5/7   Reviewed Pappas comments. Items to discuss:
   • Wants 15 year lease only 10 years is okay.
   • Wants 6 months free rent instead of 4 months (open item).
   • Says Tenant's financial condition should negate need for security. (Have CFO's office review financials.)

5/8   Redrafted lease and sent to Pappas for review with list of items rejected.

5/9   Pappas called said there are still some open items. Set up meeting for 2:00 P.M. my office on 5/10

5/10 Met with Pappas; easy to work with Insists on 15 year lease. I suggested 10 years with 5 year option at fair market rental. Security was discussed, and based on CFO's report we settled on 3 months security. All other issues resolved.

5/11 Pappas called and said client okay'd everything. Wants final draft of lease.

5/12 Sent out final draft and requested execution and checks ASAP.

5/13 Received signed leases and checks. Prepare resume of lease and submit to DJT for approval and signature. Lease signed and copies sent to Pappas with thank you note.

Keeping a detailed deal book takes a lot of time, effort, and thought, but adopting this as a work habit enables you to stop anytime and go on to other matters. When this particular negotiation heats up again, you will remember exactly where you left off. If for some reason you have to delegate the negotiation to someone else, they can pick up where you left off without missing a beat. In any line of work, the deals have many similarities though the terms and faces may change. No matter how good your memory may be, deals will tend to blend and look alike. This is a real hazard. When I was counsel for Goldman & DiLorenzo, I personally negotiated and closed 702 real estate deals in 10 years. If I hadn't developed my deal book technique, I would have been hopelessly confused and ineffectual.

The Deal Book Tracks the Points of the Deal

You should use the deal book to create a checklist of negotiation points including (1) what has been agreed to and (2) what items are still open and what is needed to solve them. This helps you to organize and track the negotiation as it moves through the process. There may be dozens of minor points to cover, and you'll lose track of them without a deal book.

You can also check out claims made by the other side. For example, the seller of a house may say, "I put on a new roof," so you write that down to check later. There are going to be many claims or statements you may want to check out. If you list those items under a "to do" list you can check them off once they are done or are deemed to be unimportant and a waste of time.

The We-They List

It always helps to keep a scorecard. So I make a side-by-side listing of each point that either is or will be under discussion to summarize the differences between the two sides. I call this the "we-they" list. By writing it down, I can see all of the areas that were in dispute or remain in dispute, and then I can prioritize the points yet to be resolved. Which ones should be disposed of immediately? Which ones are deal breakers? Which items are going to require more discussion, perhaps some suggested compromise?

For example, I want to close a deal in six months; they want to close in 30 days. This is a potentially serious dispute needing resolution before we can ultimately agree on a deal. This also identifies priorities, both for my side and for theirs.

If your list is comprehensive enough, it makes the points of disagreement finite and manageable. A seemingly insurmountable disagreement may be broken down in this way and made to seem easier to tackle. At various points during the negotiation, you can discuss the items on your list and ask the other side, "Is this everything that you want? If we resolve these items are we through?"

For the sake of argument, let's say the other side agrees that you have listed all of the open points of the deal, but much later on, they raise new issues. This can occur if the other side wants to keep changing the scope of what's being negotiated. The "we-they" checklist is invaluable for defeating this tactic. You can say, "Wait a minute, I thought you agreed that we had it all down, summarized in the list. Where did these items come from?" You may not completely win the argument, but at least the other side will have to explain their new position and they may be embarrassed in doing so. The other side may have forgotten one or two minor points, but essentially all of the unresolved material terms of the deal should be on the list. This makes it very difficult for them to add major new points at a later date. The key question arising from the list is, "If we solve all of these problems, do we have a deal?" If the answer is, "No," then find out what's missing. If the answer is, "Yes," pick out the items you want to discuss and the order in which you would like them discussed. A comprehensive deal book brings clarity to that type of discussion.

The Deal Book Also Contains a Wish List

The wish list is a summary of everything you would ideally want to achieve, not necessarily what has happened or what is going to happen. So if I want to close in six months and they want to close in 30 days, we have an unresolved issue. Knowing this, my wish list may have the entry, "Maybe I can get them down to four months if I make a larger down payment."

This works for anything that's a part of the deal and that you wish you could negotiate. You are not going to get all of what you wish for, but even the items you didn't win have surrender value so the wish list is useful in clarifying your priorities for various items requiring additional negotiation.

It's POST Time

Before you go into any negotiation remember, "It's POST time" for you and the other members of your team.

The acronym POST stands for Persons, Objectives, Strategies, and Tactics. Your deal book should include each of these items and should be completed before you enter the negotiation arena.

Persons Attending the Meeting

You need to know who is there, what their roles or level of authority is, and how do they benefit from this deal? An unidentified party is someone in attendance but you don't know who they are and what role they intend to play in the negotiation. It's possible that they're the real decision makers and, if that's a fact, your arguments should be addressed directly to them.

So let's say someone walks into the meeting room. I try to find out more, but without being too blunt. "Nice to meet you," I say, "What do you do with the company? What's your role in this discussion?" If they tell me they're attending strictly to advise someone else, now I know their role. So now I might ask, "Oh, so you're an advisor. What subject is your area of expertise? Have you been involved in many of these kinds of negotiations?" I adopt a manner in this discussion that makes me appear interested and friendly while still getting the information I want. For example, if the person tells me, "I'm here to ensure that our budget isn't exceeded," this tells me the person is a financial advisor. I ask, "Did you prepare the budget or did someone else? How did you arrive at all the line items?" I now know that I should direct dollars and cents matters to that person. I may also be able to uncover unknown limits or restrictions I didn't know existed. In addition to knowing the roles the participants will play in the negotiation, I list everything I have learned about each of them including those on my side. If someone on my side is quick with an answer, I want to muzzle him and ask him not to venture an opinion unless I ask for it. If someone is a grandstander, I have to make certain she is a team player and understands that I'm the coach and I call the plays. I also list the characteristics of the other side. I assume their attorney is there for legal advice not as a business advisor. (This is one I have to check out as the negotiations proceed.)

Objective

What is the objective of the meeting? To properly identify your objective it must be one that is measurable or attainable at the meeting. Suppose I go into a first meeting with a seller of a house. Do I intend to buy the house at this meeting? No, it's exploratory. I want to find out if it's attractive enough for me to proceed. I want to get initial information for now, and that's all. I want to reach a conclusion that I'm dealing with an honest person, someone I can trust and someone I feel comfortable with. This is a worthwhile objective.

I certainly don't want to tell the seller that I won't sign a sales contract that day. I want to play it cool and not tip my hand. If I tip my hand too soon, I won't end up with the best possible deal. So I would prefer to go in and say, for the purposes of negotiation, that I am interested in buying the house. My objective for the meeting is not to buy the house, but to determine whether I'd consider buying the house and whether it's worth my time and expense to go further.

Maybe I'll discover I'm going to have a problem when dealing with this person. I've still met my objective by eliminating that seller or that house without spending any money.

Now consider what happens if I go into the meeting without having a clear objective. (Incidentally, this is how most people go into a meeting.) Well, in that case, anything could happen. How many times have you seen someone go shopping "just to look" and end up buying a new big-screen television, or even a car or a house? If they meant only to check out the prices with the idea of making a decision at a later meeting, why did they buy instead? They went into the meeting without a clear objective and were unable to control the final outcome.

Strategies

You should plan ahead which negotiation strategy you want to use. Strategy is the decision about how to appear, demeanor, point of view—excitement, boredom, enthusiasm. So in a hot market, you don't want to appear lukewarm about the deal. You want to start out saying, "I'm ready to outbid everybody else." You might not be, but that's the tactic you use to convince the other side to listen to you. If you know there will several offers coming in on the house, you want to be seen as the most eager. In truth, you might not be willing to outbid everyone; but as long as you're still in the negotiation, you want it to appear that you are the most serious one at the table.

Another strategy is what is commonly called the "good cop/bad cop routine." That's where one member of your team indicates a desire to be cooperative and another is completely negative. An effective variation of this strategy is a reversal of roles at different stages of the negotiation. Under that scenario, the other side doesn't know who the real decision maker is. One trait of a good negotiator is a lack of predictability. This confuses the other side when they try to develop an effective game plan of their own.

Another role two people can play is that one will do all the talking and the other will be little more than a note taker. Especially in business situations, negotiators often bring someone with them. There was one case in which the owner of a securities firm had a disagreement with a wire house about a buy order that got placed as a sell order. Several thousand dollars were lost, but it was the wire house's error. So the head of the brokerage firm went to the wire house to try and negotiate with them to get the problem resolved. He took along his accountant and told him, "Wear your gray suit and a frayed tie and don't smile or say anything. When you shake hands, do it limply. Bring a legal pad and a pen, nothing else. Most important of all, every time this guy starts talking, you start writing."

Sure enough, this tactic worked and rattled the wire house executive because he felt certain he was being set up for a lawsuit. To avoid what he viewed as potentially costly litigation, he finally agreed to pay for the mistake. The note taker was a powerful weapon, and it worried the other side. (The wire house guy should have asked, "Who are you and why are you taking notes?") But people don't usually ask and if they do, they're satisfied with a weak reply.

When I'm in a negotiation, I never deal directly with the note taker. But it's important for me to know that there's a note taker there and what is said is on the record. However, I'm going to ask who the person is and why it so important to take detailed notes.

Tactics

Tactics involves the decision about who does what to implement a strategy. Who is going to be the talker and who is going to be the note taker? Who is going to be the good cop and who is going to be the bad cop? You need to plan your tactics in advance. Assume the strategy a couple decided to use was "good cop/bad cop." Let's look at the tactics that might implement such a strategy. The wife says, "I think this is a very nice house and I could see myself living there," and the husband says, "I don't think it's so great and it's far too expensive. We weren't planning an amount anything near your asking price, and I think the house is way overpriced." The wife is sounding completely enthusiastic about buying the house, but the husband is either contradicting her or remaining silent. Well, the seller or the seller's agent knows at that point that the husband has to be convinced. The agent will then concentrate on the husband. To sway the stubborn husband, there's an increased likelihood that the agent will make some concessions—which could be in price, payment of closing costs and inspection fees, or kicking in appliances or furniture. There are an infinite number of possible things the agent might consider to sweeten the deal. In this case, the husband—by remaining silent for the most part—could actually improve the deal and win concessions. This could be more effective than outright asking for them. Two people on the same side of a negotiation can effectively play off each other in that way and gain leverage against the other side. But they have to do it right; if they go too far and get to the point of just toying with the other side, negotiations will take a downhill turn or cease entirely.

REVIEW EVERY NEGOTIATION IMMEDIATELY AFTERWARD

Promptly after every negotiation meeting or phone call, you should review the outcome with the people on your side. Do this *immedi-*

ately while it's fresh in everyone's mind, and document what went on in your deal book, noting everything that happened, and indicating points you think are important. What new facts were introduced? What negotiating positions changed and why did they change? If you're under any kind of pressure, your memory will promptly fade and what occurred at that negotiating session will become a lost memory.

The prompt review is especially critical in dealing with the similar types of situations over and over again. You will get confused and make mistakes if you don't document where you are. Remember to ask yourself during this review process:

- *Was the objective achieved? If not, why not?* Why didn't we get what we wanted? Remember the old saying, "If you don't know where you're going, any road will take you there." By defining your objective ahead of time, you create the yardstick you need to measure your performance afterward. And when you don't meet your objective, you can learn from it and improve your performance next time.

- *What was good and what was bad?* What went wrong? What did I do that worked and what didn't work? What else could I have done to achieve a better result? What should we do before the next meeting? Was the timetable for proceeding within my control? There is much to be learned from any mistakes that happened, and you can use those lessons to improve your skills to overcome a similar mistake in the next meeting. This self-analysis is critical to anyone who wants to improve himself, in negotiation or any other life situation. Talk to everyone on your side who attended the meeting. Get their points of view that may differ from yours. If your demeanor was rattled by something the other side said, you need to hear criticism about that so you won't react the same way next time.

145

- *How should you revise your original assumptions?* You should always start out with certain assumptions, but be ready to modify or eliminate them after each meeting. You went in with one thought, but you came out with another. For example, I assumed that there was flexibility in a purchase price and it could be negotiated down. Now, I found out the seller is not willing to negotiate the price for the reasons he gave. My assumption about price may have to be revised if the seller can be believed. If I accept any new position, I must create a new assumption. Remember, assumptions are not facts, they are merely beliefs; they are a starting point. You need to build a series of assumptions in order to get the negotiation process rolling. But welcome the chance to revise those assumptions when additional information is obtained. The worst thing you can do is to continue operating on the wrong assumptions. The truth in all assumptions must be tested periodically. If you want to be an effective Trump-style negotiator, you must be flexible and able to change your assumptions as information develops.

- *How should you schedule and time the next meeting?* If the seller says, "I need a deal within three days or I'll do it with someone else," you need to decide why they need to fast-track the deal or if they are merely trying to put pressure on you. What's going on? If you want to accept this timeframe, you have to conclude negotiations on that schedule, but you can use this to your advantage. You might respond, "Hey, nobody works as fast as I do. I've got the money, my banker is lined up; I've got the credit; and I can pay you all cash. I'll have my lawyer call your lawyer today. I'll prepare a contract for you to review." Whatever it takes, you can turn it to an advantage. The seller's apparent need for a fast conclusion may permit you to draw up the contract, and now you have a chance to write the deal in the manner that is most favorable to you. You turn the pressure of a three-day deadline into an opportunity for you to draft all of the documents. That's a good swap.

- *What should happen to your notes?* The notes taken at any meeting must be put in your file (or deal book or computer) right away. You must keep this file up to date throughout the negotiation. It is all too easy to forget, and weeks later you are going to come upon those notes and you won't remember what the discussion was even about. You have to date the notes and organize them. They become part of your checklist of where you stand, what you agreed on, what's left. The notes are crucial to winning any negotiation.

Most negotiations go on over a long period of time involving a multiplicity of meetings at various times and under varying circumstances. I call this "transactional fractionalization," where you have a lot of negotiations in phases over things of varying importance, but they're really all part of the larger overall transaction.

After a meeting and writing up your notes, it might be appropriate to write a letter to the other side saying, "I'm so glad we were able to agree on the following items, and it convinces me we are going to be able to come to a final agreement in the near future." Now if the other side did not agree to those items, they have to come back to you and say so. However, if they just accept the letter without comment, you have a tacit approval of everything you put in the letter. It's implied consent. Now you may anticipate the possible problem by adding a statement in the letter, "If you disagree with any of these items, please let me know immediately."

If this comes up later, you can say, "I sent you a letter about this item weeks ago. If you thought that my letter was wrong, why didn't you tell me when you received it? Why bring this up now? Why are we wasting time bringing up issues we resolved before?"

By documenting the agreement to a particular date or point in the negotiation, it becomes a fact and you continue in good faith. This makes it very difficult for the other side to contradict the agreement later. It keeps you in control. I wouldn't write this kind of letter after every meeting, but in an extended negotiation, I'd pick the milestones and send a letter to update the progress of an emerging agreement or series of smaller interim agreements. You don't want the other side to think you're over-zealous and barraging them with paper. This could lead to them feeling they have to be careful about what they say. But sending a letter after every third or fourth meeting lets you summarize the items agreed to, and also what you haven't yet agreed to. This defines the status of the negotiation for both sides. The alternative—just waiting for progress to happen—does not give control over to either party. Few people take the trouble to document their discussions, so this becomes a powerful and important tool. The one who keeps good records usually wins.

II

STRATEGIES FOR
SPECIAL SITUATIONS

10

POWER NEGOTIATING
TACTICS AND
COUNTERMEASURES

THE POWER NEGOTIATING tactics described in this chapter can help you control the tone and pace of the negotiation. However, you have to be careful. If you misuse your power, it will backfire. Here's an example from my own experience that I will never forget.

In my heyday, when I was negotiating with a killer instinct, I would use any tactic that I felt would work. I was somewhat immature and thought in those days that if the best way to solve a problem was to get somebody out of the way, I would use whatever legal means were in my hands to do that. I was dealing once in a leasehold transaction with a woman lawyer on the other side. She was very bright but impossible to work with. Everything we discussed had to be done her way or no way. I could see that she was going to be a major impediment to a successful conclusion of the deal. Several times during our disagreements she became very emotional. I thought there was a possibility of exploiting those emotions to my benefit. So I started raising my voice and appeared to be getting upset. (At times, this can be a good tactic. If you yell at people they often get intimidated and become easier to deal with.) Zooming in on her body language, I could see that my macho approach was working with her. Finally, I decided that if I could bring this woman to tears I could probably get her client to change lawyers. So I used a barrage of sarcasm and kept bullying her until she started crying. Then I said to her client, "How do you expect me to negotiate with your lawyer when she is so emotional that she's crying? There must be someone else at that law firm who is rational." The client agreed and changed lawyers and the replacement was someone I could work with. My intimidation tactic worked.

Now, that's only part one of the story.

I kept the technique in the back of my mind, and later on I was again in a negotiation with a client whose lawyer was another young woman who was very sharp and who appeared to me to also be an impediment to a favorable negotiation. My success with the prior incident came back to my mind and I figured, "Well, if intimidation worked once with a young women attorney, why not do it again?" So I started down the same path, raising my voice, and so on, and very quickly, this woman said, "George, can we talk privately outside?" So I said "Sure," thinking she was going to be a pushover. We went into the hallway, and she said to me, "I know exactly what you're trying to do in there, and if you continue to pursue this route, I will cut your balls off in front of your client."

Needless to say that got my complete attention. In one single statement, she knocked the wind out of my sails and made it clear I wasn't going to be able to intimidate her. I immediately had to give up my tactic and treat her as an equal. She was even smart enough not to confront me in front of my client, so I wouldn't be humiliated or offended—and so that she wouldn't force me to fight her in front of other people. Her strategy worked. We went back into the room and had a very friendly successful negotiation brimming with mutual respect that resulted in a deal both sides found acceptable.

The first experience made me think I'd found an easy way to win through intimidation when dealing with women lawyers. It was immature, but that's the conclusion I drew. My real education came with the second experience. It taught me something about negotiation and specifically about how and when to use a power negotiating tactic. Sometimes intimidation and bullying evokes a negative reaction that hamstrings subsequent negotiations. I'll never forget what those lessons taught me. First, no single tactic works in every situation no matter what similarities exist. Second, people are as diverse as situations, and you should test the water carefully before you decide to jump in the pool. Third, some power tactics may be effective but may border on being unethical. Using them with a degree of frequency could severely damage your reputation. And fourth, every power tactic—even the ones I think work well—has an equally effective counter tactic.

This doesn't mean you will be always be able to conclude a successful negotiation without resorting to some power tactics. As I said before, modulating your voice is effective in some but not all situations. Here are a few more of the power negotiating tactics and countermeasures I've learned over the years.

THE CRUNCH: "YOU'VE GOT TO DO BETTER THAN THAT"

In any negotiation, you are likely to reach the point where a gap remains between the two sides and you aren't sure how to bridge it. One of the great techniques in this situation is called the "crunch." The beauty of this tactic is its use at the point where you have obtained what appears to be the maximum concessions the other side is willing to give, but you want to try for more without souring the negotiation. That's when the crunch is often effective. The crunch is the simple statement, "You've got to do better than that."

For example, if you are talking to a car salesperson, you might say, "I would pay $20,000 for that car." And the salesperson says, "Our price is $28,000, but I'll speak to the manager and see if he'll do better." You can use a variety of tactics to try and bring the price down closer to your level, but an $8,000 gap on a deal of this size is huge. Perhaps when the salesperson comes back, he says, "I spoke to the manager and he authorized me to sell it for $25,000. Is that okay with you?"

The crunch tactic calls for you to respond, "You've got to do better than that."

That doesn't cost you anything and, very often, if there remains room for further concessions, the other side will come back with something better. Perhaps the car salesperson has the authority to sell the car for $24,000. If he okays $24,000, you can do it again, by saying, "We're getting closer, but you've got to do better than that."

You're trying to bring someone to the point where they finally say, "That's the absolute best that I can do."

When that happens, it doesn't pay to once again say, "You've got to do better than that" because you've already used up this tactic. When the other side draws their line, you have to acknowledge that is as far as they say they are going to go. And that's the point. The crunch is a way of achieving two specific goals: First, you get a better deal. Second, you find the point where you've pressed them far enough, and they say they can't go any further. Now you have to decide to accept the deal or try another tactic such as creating a deadlock.

This doesn't mean you can't use the crunch again later in the same transaction. But in this particular discussion, it's outlived its usefulness. Most negotiations like the one I've outlined involve numerous discussion points—price, financing terms, delivery dates, extras that might be included, warranties, who pays extra costs, and so on—and each one of these points might be improved by using the crunch. Suppose the dealer agrees to give you free service up to 5,000 miles. "You've got to do better than that" can be used again. The crunch is a way of nudging the other side to work harder to find a deal that you are satisfied with.

Now you know how to use the crunch effectively, but what should you do when the other side tries to use the crunch on you? In that event, you employ a counter tactic.

If you're on the selling side of a deal and the other side tries to use the crunch on you, you counter the crunch by saying, "I've offered you a really good price, why do I have to do better than that? I've already given you a much lower price than I offer to others. Instead of my reducing the price, you should be increasing your offer."

This keeps the dialogue going but it places the pressure on the other side to respond to *your* position rather than trying to get you to change it.

Like any tactic, the crunch can be used by either side. Your advantage is that you're aware of what's happening, and most people aren't. You can use the crunch to nudge the other side's position. And when someone tries it on you, challenge it.

"THAT'S ALL I CAN DO"

The next tactic is a way of breaking off a negotiation or conversation without creating animosity. When you want to express the idea that you've negotiated as far as you're willing to negotiate and you've reached the limit of what you're willing to give, you just say, "That's all I can do. You have to make up your mind to accept my offer or not. I've gone as far as I can go."

This tactic draws the line, but in a nice way. Instead of saying "take it or leave it"—which is hostile and aggressive—you are being the nice guy while drawing the line on offering any further concessions. You aren't necessarily ending the negotiation. As a tactic, it creates the initial impression that the deal is not going to happen unless the other side capitulates. But if you're willing to talk some more, it renews the other side's hope that a deal is still possible.

What you're trying to evoke in the other side is a feeling of sympathy for your negotiation efforts. You're explaining, "I've done everything and given everything I can, but this is where I have to stop." It's almost an apology if done in this way, and it often engenders a feeling of guilt in the other side about being unable to complete the deal with you.

If someone else tries the "that's all, I can do" tactic on you, there's a good counter tactic you can use: Verify the limitation they express. So for example, you might ask, "Does this mean that under no circumstances would you be willing to reach an agreement with me on the open issues? Are you saying that you don't have the authority or that you just have decided not to budge?"

When you try to verify the limitation, it often disintegrates. So if someone tells you he can't do any more, that he can't make any further concessions, ask some pointed questions and challenge his conclusion.

Since he's taking a hard stand, you can be indignant that all the time you spent appears wasted and the least he should do is explain why he can't do anything more. Incidentally, by probing further you may discover who the final decision maker is and bring her into the negotiation.

Returning to the example of the car salesperson, what if he tells you that his boss, the sales manager, said the price is firm at $28,000. That's as low as he can go. Now you have to probe to verify that the sales manager will really say, "that's all I can do," or if there is more room to negotiate. In this kind of situation, you often find the salesperson playing the game of going to speak with the sales manager while leaving you in the office, going back and forth so that you have no idea what discussions are taking place. You're at a disadvantage. Instead, when the salesperson says, "Wait here, I'll ask my sales manager," you come back with, "Well, I'd like to talk to the sales manager directly. What's the point of you acting as a messenger?" You might insist on having both the salesperson and the manager in the same room so you can play one against the other. Or, even before that, you might pose another question to the salesperson: "If I give you a firm offer of $27,000, will you present it to your boss for approval?" If he says no, you insist, "Let me talk to the sales manager myself."

But if the salesperson says, "Yes, I'll take this offer to my boss and see what he says," that means the $28,000 price he stated previously is gone. Why would he refer your offer if he knew for a fact that $28,000 was a strict limit? His reaction tells you all you need to know. This negotiation isn't over. It's just getting started but somehow you have to get one on one with the manager if you want to make the best deal possible.

NIBBLING

If you nibble enough, you can make a meal of peanuts. Nibbling is getting something extra, something you'd like that goes beyond the agreement itself. A lot of nibbling may take place after the contract is signed. So after you buy that car and close the deal, you might say to the salesperson, "Of course, I assume that your practice is to have it washed and delivered with a full tank of gas."

In the case of a used car, perhaps you ask for a clean bill of health from the seller's mechanic or make the sale contingent on an inspection by your mechanic. But nibble by asking the seller to pay for it. A nibble often is posed as if the request was a given, unspoken but understood—and now you're just verifying that this was intended all along.

Another nibble is when a home buyer says, "I know that you're leaving me the lawn furniture but I would like the tools in the garage since they really should go with the house." The nibbling possibilities in many negotiations are endless.

It's not unethical to ask for extras. You are not insisting on getting the extra concession, just making a request. As long as I ask in a nice way, no harm is done. After the contract has been signed, I can no longer say, "If you don't give me these little things that I'm asking for, I'm not going to honor the deal."

Once the parties have signed a contract and everything has been finalized, it is unethical for the seller to come back and say, "I want more money" or for the buyer to say "I want to pay less." That's not a nibble. With a signed contract, you can't ethically try to unilaterally change the terms of the agreement. There is an effective counter tactic to be used against the nibbler. If someone tries to nibble in a deal I'm making, I can handle it or neutralize it. I put a price on the nibble. So if you're buying a car from me and you say you want the car washed and filled with gas, I say, "Sure I'll do that, but the car wash will cost you an additional $30 and the gas is $50 more. I'll do those things for $80." In the case of the lawn furniture, my response to the nibble would be, "I need it at my new house but if you really want it, I'll sell it to you for a reasonable price."

Nibbling is an accepted practice in many cultures. In my experience, I have found some people are extremely adept in using this tactic in their negotiations.

The Change of Pace

If you have a situation where there has been a lot of fast-moving discussion and back-and-forth concessions, it's a good tactic to change the pace by digging in your heels on something you are really willing to give up at a later date. This slows down the whole process while placing you in control of the progress of the negotiation. When you change your tactics, the other side can't read you as being all yes or all no, all slow or all fast. If you constantly cave in on issues, they won't believe you when you stand firm. You have a distinct advantage in knowing that a change of pace will keep the other side off balance. This is a power tactic for you to use. If the other side cannot detect a pattern in your style, they are at a loss to create a winning strategy.

Another way to change the pace is by throwing something into the mix that was never a part of the original transaction. You change the pace long enough to argue about this point and then, if, reluctantly, you have to give it up, that's fine. The intention was not to win the point but to change the pace of the negotiation and add to the topics that are under discussion. That was your real purpose.

So let's say I'm coming to the end of a discussion about buying a car. I want to slow down the pace, so I say to the salesperson, "You should give me a warranty on all parts and labor for 10 years." The salesperson argues that he can't give that to you, and he isn't authorized by the dealer to include such a warranty.

I don't expect that the dealership is going to give me a warranty that broad, so perhaps I could revise the request and ask for a limited warranty beyond the one offered by the manufacturer. I've bargained away one idea that I knew I could never win, and that was never a part of the discussion of the price, but I've brought up another idea for the dealership to consider. So if the dealership won't do that either, I might say, "Well, if you won't give me a warranty, you should take $1,000 off the price to cover my risk."

I might end up with something extra, or I might not. But I've managed to change the pace, slow down the discussion, and give myself time to think the deal through and make sure I'm ready to sign off. Either way, the pace is now in my control.

Now what should you do if someone tries to change the pace on you? The counter tactic here is to question what the other side is doing. I would say, "What caused you to change your style? We were getting along famously and now you're throwing a monkey wrench in the machinery. What gives? Our discussions were going great; we were making real headway toward a final agreement. Now you want to delay it for a week. Why is that?"

There could be a good explanation. If there's been a death in the family, or a medical problem, for example, it makes sense to break off the negotiation. It's important for you to find out what it was that caused the change. It could be that they're getting cold feet or have another buyer, a better deal, and so on. If the other side uses the change of pace tactic, you must challenge it. Don't let them control the pace without your approval.

"Take It or Leave It"

When you say, "take it or leave it," that's a real ultimatum. Those are fighting words, and when someone hears them, their first inclination is to leave it because no one likes to be forced into making a decision against their will. You should find a way to communicate the same message in a less belligerent manner unless you're willing to risk ending further negotiations right then and there.

To eliminate the feeling of offending someone, use the aura of legitimacy or the "I have other offers" argument. You tone down what you're saying. I might tell a buyer, "To tell you the truth, I have two other people offering me the price I stated. I'm giving you a chance to match the deal I've been offered by them if you want it." It's a logical argument.

You can also add an aura of legitimacy by saying, "The other offers are back in my office if you want to see them." If they call your bluff, you can say they were misplaced but you'll find them. Meanwhile, they must make an immediate decision, which is what happens in a "take it or leave it" scenario.

Leave a Way Out for Face Saving

In any negotiation, it rarely is a good idea to corner the other side. The single exception is when you have been lied to or there was an intentional misrepresentation. Then nailing them to the wall is okay. Otherwise, consider that you might want to come back later and reopen discussions. If you're buying my house and you say, "The most I'll pay for the house under any circumstances is $300,000, not a penny more. That's my final offer, take it or leave it." Now you cannot come back without losing face. However, if you say, "The price is higher than what I want to pay. If you won't lower it, let's think it over and maybe one of us will change his mind." Whoever comes back and re-opens the negotiations will then need to throw a concession on the table for the other side to consider.

How to Counter a "Take It or Leave It" Statement

If someone in a negotiation says "take it or leave it" to you, try to change the parameters of the discussion. If I say, "The price for my house is $350,000, take it or leave it." You may want to pay only $310,000 but to continue the negotiations you change the parameters by saying, "I might meet your price but you have to throw in some additional benefits that are worth the extra $40,000. How about taking back a purchase money mortgage on reasonable terms?"

Now you've changed the parameters of the discussion and kept the possibility open that you might buy my house if some adjustment is made in an area other than price. This moves the negotiation away from "take it or leave it" and toward "let's talk about how we can make this work."

You can also use this kind of alternative offer as a way to come back in and restart the negotiation that stopped because you took the "take it or leave it" route. You call me back up and say, "You know, I think I might agree to pay the $350,000 you asked for, but I need some financing help from you. If you're willing to carry some paper for it, we can still make a deal."

FORCED REVISIONS

One tactic to be avoided is the forced revision that happens when one side chooses to change something it has already agreed to. A forced revision will destroy any feeling of trust and friendship that has been built up during the negotiation, and turns a negotiation into a one-way demand. The prospect of a forced revision raises several questions.

Is It Ethical to Rescind a Prior Agreement on Any Item Prior to Closing?

As long as the agreement is final, rescinding it might create ill will, but until you sign, everything is still on the table. It's not unethical to continue negotiating everything and anything before the contract is signed. There is an important distinction between changing a deal before it is signed and a forced revision.

It's also important to make a distinction between acting ethically and acting unethically. Here's an example of a forced revision:

> Let's say I take my car in to a mechanic because it has a bad transmission. The mechanic quotes me $350, and I give the go-ahead. The mechanic calls up the next day and says, "I took a close look at your transmission and I can't fix it for $350. If you want it fixed, my price is $700."
>
> Now I would say, "Wait a minute. You quoted me $350, now you're changing it to $700. Forget the whole deal."
>
> So the mechanic says, "Okay, come and pick up your car, but the pieces of your transmission are all over the floor."
>
> I can't drive the car and I don't want to have it towed to another transmission place where I will be at someone else's mercy. What am I going to do? I have no choice. If I want the car, I have to pay the $700. I have every right to be irate, but this is a forced revision because I'm left with no choice. The price was raised because I had no alternative.

That's totally unethical on the part of the mechanic, and it may form the basis for litigation in those states that require mechanics to be bound by written estimates. If I'm so inclined, I can also sue the mechanic later for the overcharge. Of course, you'll never use the mechanic again and warn your friends about his shady tactics. But you're still out the additional $350.

A forced revision can be used in many situations. If one side knows the other side is irrevocably committed to a deal and has no other viable alternative, a forced revision works.

I was required to use a forced revision in a real estate deal. My client, a builder, entered into a lease that was poorly drafted by another lawyer. The tenant under the lease was a major retailer and the lease required the builder to build a store in a particular shopping center location by a given date. But after preparing the site and starting the foundation, the mortgage lender refused to make the required loan because the rent payable by the retailer was too low and some of the provisions of the lease were unacceptable to the lender. Although the lease had been drafted by my client's in-house counsel, the burden of solving this problem was placed on my shoulders. I contacted the retailer's attorney and told him that unless the rent was raised and the lease was drafted to make it acceptable to the lender, my client would not build the store. This posed a real problem for the retailer who had given up negotiating on another site and had purchased all its merchandise for this store. I told the retailer's attorney, "Your client can sue my client now for breach of lease or if your client wants the store on time, it will have to give up its right to sue and modify the lease to satisfy the lender." The retailer was furious and rightly so, but made a business decision to go along with it to get the store.

Since time was of the essence, I called Kurt Lore, the lender's knowledgeable and highly respected attorney, to find out what provisions of the lease needed revision. Kurt and I had worked on many deals and shared mutual respect and admiration. He said, "George, I have neither the time nor the inclination to tell you what I need and don't tell me you prepared that lease—it's a piece of garbage. I know your work when I see it. You know what I need and if you get it to me, I'll move quickly to get the lender's approval."

When I told the retailer's counsel that I was going to redraft the lease in its entirety and make it palatable to both landlord and tenant, he went ballistic and said, "For three months I fought over that lease with your client's in-house lawyer and now you're saying it's being scrapped? I won't agree to that!" I said, "Take it up with your client and if he wants the store it's this way or no way." The retailer overruled his attorney. I redrafted the lease using a form that had previously been approved by Kurt Lore, while keeping intact many of the benefits the retailer had originally received from my client. There was no room for negotiation, so I told the tenant's attorney, "Take it or leave it." His client said, "take it" and the new lease was signed and the lender made the required mortgage loan on the building. Needless to say, my client made some enemies in this transaction. He and the retailer ceased doing business for several years until the pain became a distant memory.

When someone tries a forced revision on you after the contract is signed, they create both an ethical and a legal problem. You have to make the hard choice between litigation and going along with what amounts to highway robbery. There is really no other option available. You can try the threat of future legal action or complaining to the better business bureau or a governmental entity, but since you're dealing with an unscrupulous person these threats will have little or no effect.

What Is the Effect on the Other Side When a Forced Revision Is Imposed?

The further along you are in the negotiation, the greater the effect and the animosity. From that point on, you must watch the perpetrator closely to minimize the loss. You know that he cannot be trusted any longer.

Take note that in some cultures, it is considered business as usual to try to force a better deal *after* signing the contract. If you're dealing with someone known to employ these tactics, there is no basis for any trust, friendship or mutual satisfaction. They're going to chisel at the last moment, and it's just a question of how much and how you want to handle it. Being unethical about honoring an agreement ends up affecting a person's reputation, but that type of person cares only about the immediate dollars, not his reputation. As a matter of fact, he believes that his ability to successfully chisel late in the game is a badge of honor. If you decide to make a deal with a known chiseler, be sure you left yourself enough room to pay for the chisel maneuver.

11

NEGOTIATING WITH DIFFICULT PEOPLE

I T WOULD BE a nice world if we had to negotiate only with friendly, honest people who did not play mind games with us. But, unfortunately, that is not how things work in the real world. I have often had to contend with people who made things unpleasant or difficult, but over the years I've figured out the best way to deal with them. Each difficult person has some area of vulnerability. Once you identify how to strategically maximize your position with that vulnerability in mind, you can gain the negotiating advantage, even with the most difficult person. I have broken down the major difficult character types into three broad categories that I discuss in this chapter.

Ivan the Intimidator

The first type you're likely to encounter at some time or another is a bully. Usually the intimidator is male; maybe it's a macho thing. If he can get away with cowing you into submission and giving in to him, he will do it. But as it is true with all bullies, there is always a way to handle this situation.

Ivan the Intimidator is usually someone with stature or position who wields a great deal of power in the negotiation. Just as a schoolyard bully intimidates other kids because he is bigger than them, the negotiating bully uses any combination of his physical appearance, voice, reputation, or position to control how *you* react to him. Looking down from his perceived high vantage point, he intimidates and controls you for the sole purpose of dominating throughout the course of the entire negotiation.

The source of this power may be merely physical; a person who is very large in stature may realize that by size alone he intimidates other people. An exceptionally tall person with a booming voice can easily dominate because he is both taller and louder than everyone around him. Such a person learned early on that he could use these physical attributes to dominate others. It is rare to meet a tall, muscular, loud person who is meek. This doesn't mean such people have to be bullies, but even the nicest tall people tend to be more extroverted than average.

My first meeting with an Ivan the Intimidator occurred early in my career. It was the first time I met Bill Zeckendorf in connection with the Graybar Building leasehold purchase that was discussed in an earlier chapter. He was considered the most talented real estate person in New York at that time. Everybody knew who he was and how big a shadow he cast. His reputation as a prime wheeler and dealer gave him the ability to intimidate sight unseen.

I had never met him before, but we were negotiating a deal on the Graybar Building and my client, Sol Goldman, had put up a $400,000 deposit toward the purchase of the leasehold. I was waiting in Zeckendorf's offices to get an itemized rent roll. Usually this is not a big deal; it's a standard document that sellers provide to buyers in connection with the sale of an office building. It usually consists of a listing of all the tenants, when their leases expire, monthly rent, and other important information. I had been promised the rent roll by Zeckendorf's three attorneys.

Suddenly the office door opened and in walked Zeckendorf. Although we had never met before, he looked me right in the eye and said, "Young man, I understand your client is about to lose $400,000 because of your insistence on the rent roll." That was his opening salvo. Standing silently behind him were three lawyers.

Unwittingly, he had made a big mistake by calling me young man. I was very sensitive about my youthful appearance that others sometimes equated with a lack of experience. I did look young, but I'd been practicing law for several years and had developed considerable experience in the field of real estate. To me, it was as though he'd called me "shrimp." As a pure reflex reaction, I said to him, "I assume from the fact that your entourage has said absolutely nothing and is standing there behind you like 'speak no evil,' 'hear no evil,' and 'see no evil,' that you must be Bill Zeckendorf."

He merely nodded. Finally, he said, "If you insist on getting that rent roll, the deal's over and I'm going to keep the $400,000 deposit. You can leave right now."

Bristling at his arrogance, I replied, "I was told by your lawyers that they would give me the rent roll today." At this point, the three lawyers became the three monkeys—hear no evil, see no evil, speak no evil—protesting in unison, "I never told him that!" Zeckendorf then repeated his threat, "Well, if you insist on getting it, I'm saying you can leave right now."

I had reached my boiling point and responded irately, "I don't represent you, Mr. Zeckendorf. I represent Sol Goldman, he can tell me when and if I stay or go! I will call Sol and ask him what he wants me to do. And in my opinion, if you really thought you could keep the $400,000, you'd do it. You wouldn't even be talking to me."

His response was to turn and storm out of the room followed by his cohorts. I called Sol Goldman and he waived the requirement for the rent roll.

Zeckendorf was trying to intimidate me, and it didn't work. I knew we could work around the absent rent roll document, but I wasn't going to tell Zeckendorf that. His refusal to hand it over puzzled me at the time because it was a minor document. After I attained more negotiation experience, I realized he was testing me to see how I would react to severe pressure from him. It wasn't long before I found out what he thought of my performance.

The next day, Zeckendorf called me. He started out the conversation saying in an extremely friendly manner, "George, how are you?"

I thought for a brief moment and then I replied, "Bill, I'm fine. How are you?" Just one day after the opening hostilities, we were now on a first-name basis!

Zeckendorf said, "I have Sol with me here in my office and I have a document ready for his signature. Sol says he won't sign anything unless you approve it. Is it okay with you if I have it read to you now so that you can advise your client whether or not to sign?" Now that he needed me for something, honey could have dripped out of his mouth. When I heard the contents of the document, I knew it was innocuous and I told Sol to sign it.

The point here is that when you look at a powerhouse personality you may see intimidation at one point and then the complete opposite the next. This is typical of an intimidator. They change like night and day depending on what *they* need or the atmosphere they want to create at the moment. In this case, Zeckendorf also discovered that the steamroller tactic didn't work with me, so he went to plan B, which was being nice.

You have great power in working with Ivan the Intimidator by recognizing how the ploy works. The whole idea is to intimidate, so if you don't let that work, they have to go to plan B. Since plan B is to win you over, it gives you a great advantage. They *want* to please you because they want to believe they're still in control. They convince themselves that being nice (or at least pretending to be nice) will get you eating out of the palm of their hand. A major flaw in Ivan the Intimidator is that very few of his actions are sincere. He plays various roles at different times, but he really doesn't know how to get a favorable action from people by acting normally.

Some advice for working with Ivan the Intimidator follows.

Be Low-Key but Stand Your Ground

I didn't choose to escalate the initial confrontation with Zeckendorf, but I did remind him, "I don't work for you." I was letting him know he couldn't intimidate me. I was standing my ground, and showing him that I was not at all intimidated by his posturing.

This is hard to do; it's easy to become flustered when someone with power or prestige becomes confrontational. No one is more confrontational than Ivan the Intimidator. He automatically starts testing you by using the steamroller approach, just to see whether you will lie down quietly and be run over. If it works, then he knows the tactic is effective and he'll use it constantly. But if it doesn't work, two things will change immediately. First, there will be different tactics used to achieve the result he wants. Second, control of the situation has shifted from him to you.

Establish Rapport, but Not on the Battlefield

In this case, Zeckendorf established rapport with me by making the telephone call in a friendly manner. If he hadn't done so, and I had to continue dealing with him, I would have had to figure out a way to smooth things over. He did it first. He leveled the playing field. The important thing to remember when dealing with an intimidator is *never* do anything that will diminish his stature in the eyes of his subordinates. Private talks, cocktails, or a one-on-one setting is the way to get his cooperation in facilitating the deal.

Ivan will often to establish rapport with you as soon as he realizes that the steamroller tactic will not work. He might try to become your friend, flatter you, or figure out some other way to "neutralize" you in the negotiation. When Ivan's absence hinders the negotiations, you have to take steps to establish some rapport because the advantage has shifted to you, it is important for you to hold onto it. Something like a telephone conversation in which you say, "I know we got off on the wrong foot, but we both want to get the deal done, so let's work everything out."

I did go further to create rapport later in the same phone call. I told Zeckendorf, "Bill, I will never ask for anything more than I would be willing to give if I were on the other side. If you tell your lawyers to be cooperative, they will find that I'm an easy guy to work with. Then we can both operate with a view toward finishing the transaction as soon as possible."

When you appeal to Ivan with that kind of reasoning, your arguments are compelling. You're asking the general to control his troops. Ivan might believe that he is winning when you make the first move to establish rapport. That doesn't matter; let him think he's winning. As long as the outcome is that you get the cooperation you need to complete the deal, that's all that matters.

Institute Constant Monitoring to Avoid Incursions

After we had established rapport, I had a direct line to Zeckendorf. Because he had decided that we were friends, I could call on him whenever I needed help. This gave me great leverage with his lawyers. If they did something I didn't like, I'd threaten to call Bill and get him to straighten things out. Usually the threat was enough to get them to change their thinking. My experience has led me to the conclusion that the person who likes to use intimidation hates reading documents. He doesn't like details, he expects his staff to handle that. He prefers to enter a room with a grand gesture and then sweep out with a fanfare, his entourage in tow. Then you never see or hear from him except in a crisis. So another very effective way to manage this type of personality is to flood him with details that he will never read but, you can say you kept him informed on everything.

For example, every time I sent a document to one of Zeckendorf's lawyers, I'd send a copy to him. In a major real estate transaction, there are hundreds of documents going back and forth. If nothing else, real estate is complex because of the paperwork. And real estate deals have to be in writing, so the documentation is critical.

What did I accomplish when I copied every single document to Zeckendorf? First of all, it scared the lawyers because they knew their boss could assess their actions. It meant if they made a misstep the boss might come down on them like a ton of bricks. Second, if something came up later and the lawyers said, "we never agreed to that," I could always reply, "I advised you about that three weeks ago and Zeckendorf never objected to it."

If later Zeckendorf said that he never agreed to something, I would tell him, "Bill, I raised this issue weeks ago and neither you nor your people said a word about it. Now, at the last minute, you raise this issue?" I may not win the point, but the other side is now on the defensive. The paper barrage keeps you in control because, even though Ivan is the Intimidator, he himself is intimidated by the myriad of details that abound in any complex transaction.

Know-It-All Charlie

You've probably heard the expression, "No one likes a know-it-all." Well, that's true in negotiation as much as it is anywhere else. There still seems to be many know-it-alls out there. It is entirely possible for you to come up against someone with a tremendous amount of personal or professional experience, or who has a recognized name and stature in the industry. This person is difficult to deal with because he believes that he really does know everything about the transaction you're contemplating. The more well-known someone becomes and the more successful deals he has completed, the more hubris sets in; and this is the key to dealing with the know-it-all.

The minute you begin talking, he is going to tell you, "I've been down this road hundreds of times. I was doing this before you were born, and I know all the arguments you're going to make. So don't try to tell me what I should or should not do. I already know what needs to be done." Once he exhibits that attitude, you have gained an advantage. Don't ever think like that; it could be hazardous to your negotiating health. There is something to be learned from every person you talk to and from every deal you work on. You never stop learning and picking up information that often proves useful. When teaching my negotiating classes at NYU, I give my students my address, and telephone and fax numbers, and I encourage them to call me when they have a sticky negotiation problem. Many students of past years call me to tap my brain. I also tap theirs to see if there's some bit of information I can glean from the conversation. I tell them to let me know if my advice was useful, and I store their response in my database for future recall if necessary. The flaw that the know-it-all suffers from is that he has stopped believing that there's more to learn. He truly believes he knows everything about the topic. You can use that conceit to your advantage.

Exhibit Extreme Humility

The first tactic for you to employ is an exhibition of extreme humility. When someone tells you, "I'm the expert," a good response would be, "Yes, I know that. I've read your work, and I've talked to people who have dealt with you and they sing your praises." Flattery with the know-it-all gets you anywhere you want to go. You feed his ego when you acknowledge the extent of his expertise. He believes that you see him as the authority, and therefore this negotiation is going to be a slam dunk for him.

Once the know-it-all thinks you are convinced of his superiority, his guard goes down. We can all learn a lot from the fable "The Tortoise and the Hare." The Hare was so fast he knew he could easily win the race, so he fell asleep and lost to the Tortoise who just kept plodding along. In essence, the know-it-all falls asleep as soon as he becomes convinced that *you* know and accept that he has superior knowledge. As soon as you become subservient, the know-it-all relaxes and assumes that he has already won. Now, the know-it-all's big ego might be justified by his experience, but couple that with your humble acceptance of his position and he is off guard, and that's when you can seize the opportunity to gain the advantage.

Give Minimal Information and Many "You Know" Statements

Know-it-all Charlie might be considered to be the most arrogant personality type you will encounter in a negotiation. However, if you keep focused on what you want to accomplish, you can use his own ego and smugness to enable you to run circles around him.

The last thing you want to do is get in a head-to-head argument. Because the know-it-all knows more than you and is far superior, he will never let you win an argument. In fact, challenging him directly will only infuriate him and make it impossible to get to a point of agreement. Instead, you want to stroke his ego in order to gain concessions.

When you have a particular point that you want to win, don't go into great detail. And don't try to sell it. Instead of trying to get agreement to a clause in contract, just say, "You know what is typical on this issue. You've done this a thousand times. Let me send you the language you're familiar with and we'll use that."

When he gets your language, it may vary from "typical," but the know-it-all would never admit he's never seen the deviation before. That would make him seem less than perfect in his overall knowledge, so it is more likely that he will agree with you. He is likely to listen to what you're saying, but he doesn't pay close attention to nuances and assumes he's only hearing that which he has heard a hundred times before. His unbridled ego triggers a lack of concentration.

What if Know-it-all Charlie does challenge you? He might say, "What do you mean by saying this is typical? This is anything but typical." Now what?

A good come-back would be to ask, "Well you've got much more experience and knowledge than I do, can you tell me what you think is typical? Based on your extensive expertise, how would you word this clause?" This allows the know-it-all to show off his knowledge. Chances are good that his bottom line is going be a mere matter of semantics. The know-it-all is not motivated by the details. He simply wants to be acknowledged as *the* expert. Let him do the talking and see where it goes.

A wise approach with this person, even in the face of a challenge, is to say, "Just give me what you would want yourself in this kind of agreement and I'll accept that. You know what I need."

At this point, I haven't told him exactly what I want. I want to hear what he's willing to give me. The last thing I want to do is to challenge his authority because this is his entire claim to fame and identity. Since I've assumed a subservient position, he won't view me as a tough negotiator or as a threat to him. I use his aura of power and knowledge against him, but that gives me an advantage.

Solicit Help in Dealing with His Side

Get somebody on his side to help you when you're trying to make a point. Usually, the know-it-all does not want to get involved in all of the details of the negotiation, so he relies on others. If you can convince the people on that level to listen to what you're saying, and write it down, then you can use them to convince the know-it-all. For example, you can say, "Why don't you have one of your underlings take this up with your boss? I'm sure he knows how to resolve this issue. He'll tell you that what I'm asking for is typical since he's probably done it almost as many times as you have."

He will take your message to the boss and deliver a response back to Know-it-all Charlie. You can take it from there. If a meeting with the boss is needed, schedule one to get Charlie off the hook.

Waffling Wilma

This is a person who has difficulty making decisions. That's the hardest kind of person to deal with because you never know where you stand and, even when you think you do, you're probably wrong. If she says "yes" it might be yes for the minute, but an hour later she might contradict herself.

She is also prone to say, "This sounds good, but I'll have to think about it."

She never wants to make a final decision about anything and if forced to finally make any decision at all, she'll try to figure out some way to avoid being bound by it. If it becomes easier to say no than yes, she will say no. Waffling Wilmas are simply not confident about making final decisions.

Go Slowly and Be Patient

You need to move steadily forward with Waffling Wilma, making sure you don't let her take you backward to revisit yesterday's topic. If you've discussed something and it's agreed on, move forward. You also need to define where you are. You need to say, "We started with five points, and agreed on three. Now we have the remaining two."

If she disagrees with this summary, then you need to determine where the indecision or disagreement resides and get that resolved. Then you move forward. It's slow, but by defining what has been accomplished, you can finally get through it.

It might be useful in dealing with Waffling Wilma to summarize now and then with a brief letter. In this letter, you list the points discussed and the agreements you both made. This tactic can go either way. If she disputes any of the points you raise, then you do need to go back and get them resolved. If she agrees or simply doesn't respond, then you can proceed to the next matter.

Most people don't bother to reply to clarifying written summaries. But if anyone will bring up the same topics again later, it's Waffling Wilma. But with the letter behind you, it is reasonable to say, "Wait a minute. We agreed to this already. I sent you a letter and you never said a word. Why are you bringing it up again now?"

Some cultural traditions may result in a Waffling Wilma situation. If your negotiator needs to get final approval from someone else, the agreement could be reversed or contradicted. So whether it's a character flaw or a cultural reality, you deal with someone with this personality in the same way—with patience.

Build Up Her Stature with Her Side

If you've been negotiating with someone and all of a sudden she backtracks, you may need to go to her superiors—the real decision makers in this case—and tell them what a great job their negotiator is doing.

You're making the person look good in front of the boss. This helps everyone, and hopefully the boss will then give her a little more free rein based on you telling him that his representative is doing such a great job protecting his interests. Remember, Waffling Wilma starts out with an inferiority complex, so this strategy allows the negotiation to move forward. To the extent that you can bolster her self-confidence—which she lacks—you can only improve the situation. When you let her superiors know what a great job Waffling Wilma is doing, it also tends to ally her with you more closely. You can turn her from an adversary into a partner, equally interested in making the deal happen.

Be Stingy with Concessions

Giving up anything to Waffling Wilma is likely to only cause even more indecision. The more you give her, the more confused she becomes. So when you're talking about alternatives, don't offer plans A, B, C, and D or you'll never get an answer. Start out with the one you'd prefer. "Here's the plan I propose we follow" is preferable to "Which of these four do you like?" When you propose plan A, tell her "This is the best alternative for both of us. It's simple, it's obvious, and we both get what we want." Don't offer details. If she has questions, let her ask them. Prod her to agree and see how that goes. If she turns the idea down completely, then you can go to plan B, but only then. Remember, the more choices you put before Waffling Wilma, the thinner your chances are of getting a yes on anything.

By nature, Waffling Wilma is not a decision maker. So you have a better negotiating position to propose solutions, argue for them, and convince her they make sense.

These three personality types are not restricted as to gender. The types can be male or female. Some people exhibit a combination of these difficult traits at the same time. Ivan the Intimidator may also be a Know-it-all Charlie, for example. And Know-it-all Charlie might impress his superiority throughout the negotiations, only to turn into Waffling Wilma at decision time. So you need to be prepared to shift from one set of tactics to another, depending on the personality you're dealing with at a particular time.

Dealing with difficult people is like trying to get kids to eat their vegetables. You might have to hide the peas inside the pasta shells to succeed, and it's irritating to deal with players who are more interested in how they play the game than the final result. People with these kinds of personalities are everywhere and, when you meet them, you're in for an experience you will never forget.

On the flip side of this discussion, a good negotiator can choose to adopt any or all of these traits when it's advantageous to do so. So while you will observe these traits as usually belonging to difficult people, they can also be useful tools for you to use at times since difficult people often get their way. I have always maintained that two-year-olds are the best negotiators. If they don't get what they want, they lie on the floor kicking and screaming until their parent says, "Okay, just stop crying and I'll give you what you want." But what happens when the parent decides to let the infant scream until he or she realizes it won't work. When that happens, the tot tries something else until he or she finds something that works. In contrast, inexperienced negotiators tend to have just one style that has worked for them in the past. So when they find themselves in a situation where that style isn't working, they're helpless. Don't let this happen to you.

I don't think too many people intentionally take on these traits. In other words, difficult people don't see themselves as being difficult. Ivan the Intimidator describes himself as merely assertive and dynamic. Know-it-all Charlie sees himself as successful and seasoned. And Waffling Wilma has a self-image of a thorough person who does not like to make mistakes. Once you understand that these are personality traits they have developed over time, it becomes quite easy to know how to deal with them.

Remember that in most situations, these traits are unconscious and the people using them see their traits as positive attributes. When you are able to turn what they perceive as attributes into a weapon you can use to improve your negotiating position, you are in command. You might prefer to have only one straightforward negotiating style with which you feel comfortable. . . . But that is just not a realistic approach if you want to become a skilled negotiator. Just as parents learn that no two children respond in the same way, you become the most effective negotiator when you're able to adjust your style from time to time when it is necessary to manage people on the other side.

12

GET TOUGH
STRATEGIES . . . AND
WHEN TO USE THEM

THE LONGER YOU practice your skills as a negotiator, the greater your chances of running into situations where getting-tough is your best alternative. I don't encourage anyone to use the "get-tough strategy" (let's call it GTS for short) in every situation, because it isn't always appropriate. But it can be very effective.

Many years ago, there was an expensive apartment building in New York that was owned by Lord Astor. He was an extremely wealthy, society icon who many people of course found intimidating. He was represented by a very large, prestigious law firm. My client, Sol Goldman, wanted to buy the building from Lord Astor.

I was going over the contract with Lord Astor's attorney when I said, "There's no representation that the rent roll is accurate. If my client is going to pay top dollar for the property, I'm going to need verification of rental income the property generates."

"No, we're not going to represent the accuracy of a rent roll," the lawyer shot back at me.

This was unheard of. It would be like buying a car without knowing how many miles are on it, or what model year it was. So I thought I would come back to this later. I started bringing up other items in the contract and suggesting revisions I wanted. The lawyer stopped me cold. "No," he said, "You can't make any changes at all. You'll just have to tell your client to sign the contract as it is. When that's done and you give me the down payment, I will send the signed contract to Lord Astor, who is on his yacht traveling in the Mediterranean at the moment. When he ties up in port, *he* will decide whether to sign the contract and sell the building. And that is how and when you will know whether you have a deal. Your client will just have to wait until you hear from us. If your client doesn't like these conditions, so be it."

So I called Goldman and I told him what Lord Astor's lawyer had said and what they wanted him to do. Sol, in his inimitable fashion, said, "I want you to go back to that lawyer and tell him you spoke to me and I said and you should quote me, 'Sol Goldman says that Lord Astor can take the contract and put it where the sun doesn't shine'."

I went back and conveyed Goldman's message word for word to Lord Astor's attorney who didn't bat an eye, but as you can imagine that ended our meeting. I thought the deal was over and done, but about a month went by, and Astor's broker came back to reopen our discussions. We ended up buying the property for *less* money than our original offer, and with all of the changes we wanted in the contract.

By refusing to compromise or respond to the other side's heavy-handed tactics, we prevailed. It was appropriate to respond the way Goldman did because the other side was trying to dictate untenable terms. . . . This is a good example of when and how to use a get-tough strategy. When we knew the deal wasn't going to happen because of the impossible terms imposed by the seller, we had nothing to lose and everything to gain by showing we could be just as tough. By not caving in, we got a better deal later.

What You Should Do When You Decide to Use the Get-Tough Strategy

Of course every situation is going to present nuances and variations on the discussions, and you have to determine exactly how tough you want to get with the other side. I recommend 10 specific strategies and guidelines:

1. Set the tone.
2. Don't talk.
3. Manage concessions properly.
4. Aim high.
5. Leave as much room as possible.
6. Don't succumb to the power of the simple solution.
7. Bargain small items for big ones.
8. Use deadlines to your advantage.
9. Be patient and stingy.
10. Be careful in how you request a variation.

Let me explain each of these in a little more detail:

1. *Set the tone.* The message in Goldman's response to Astor's lawyer was appropriate. The other side set the tone—nasty, heavy-handed, and far from a give-and-take—and so we responded in like manner. We used the GTS. The message: We don't like the way you're willing to do business. This is unfair. But, since you have set this tone, we'll play by your rules. If you want to be tough, we're going to show you that we can be just as tough.

For whatever reasons, the other side might not have been keen on dealing with Sol Goldman. But I was focused on the deal. I realized that whether they liked it or not, they'd take Goldman's money for the building if his was the best offer they had. It really doesn't matter how you get to a completed transaction as long as you get there. You can complete a deal using many different tones. It is always more pleasant if you can have a friendly, sincere discussion with people. As I pointed out earlier, there are a lot of different personalities out there, so you have to be prepared to set or adapt to the tone in a negotiation. In that particular case, Astor's people might have come to the realization that they were asking too much for the building and that they weren't able to find another buyer at that price. Maybe they felt that the market was getting soft. I'll never know the reasons, but they don't matter. We got a better deal when we used the GTS than we would have gotten by playing Mr. Nice Guy.

It is important for you to be in control whenever possible. It's better if *you* can set the tone. But if you start out as Mr. Nice Guy and the other side gets nasty, then your friendly tone is not going to work and you have to change gears. If the other side sets a negative tone, don't fight it. Play by their rules and don't let them intimidate you.

2. *Don't talk. Don't explain.* When using the GTS, the less said by you or others on your side, the better you'll come out. The side that does the most talking is at a disadvantage in the negotiation because they tip their hand.

Once you have decided to use the GTS, you must indicate a willingness to stand or fall on that position. Don't explain it.

On one specific occasion, Sol Goldman taught me a GTS lesson I will never forget. Goldman had contracted to buy an apartment house and had posted a $250,000 deposit with the seller. Although the closing was only three weeks away, Sol had decided to lose his deposit and walk away from the deal. He put his contract up for sale, and a broker brought in a syndicator who would take over the contract and pay Goldman $750,000, which would net him a profit of $500,000. At the meeting in my office to assign the contract to the syndicator, an unexpected $20,000 cost arose. The sydicator said he would pay half if Goldman would pay the other half. I went into Sol's office and asked him what I should do. He said, "George, you know that I can piss away $10,000 in five minutes, but if I show any weakness the sydicator will negotiate forever. I don't have time for it. I want you to go back inside and tell him that I won't take a nickel off the price." I said, "Sol, you may blow a $250,000 deposit and a $500,000 profit for $10,000, do you think that's smart?" He replied, "Just do what I say and tell the syndicator he has five minutes to make up his mind or to get out of your office." I went back to my office and told the syndicator exactly what Goldman told me to say. The syndicator was incensed at Goldman's reaction and said, "Do you mean to tell me that your client is willing to pass up a $500,000 profit for a measly $10,000?" I replied, "That's exactly what I mean, and you have five minutes to agree or to leave my office." I left my office to spend the longest five minutes of my life. When I returned to my office, the syndicator said he would take the deal and swallow the entire $20,000 cost. After that, the negotiation was easy. Now that I knew how badly the sydicator wanted the deal, I could say "no" to anything he wanted.

Once you have decided on a GTS don't explain your reasons and give the other side an opportunity to pick them apart. Just stand pat and let the other side do all the talking. A GTS requires a certain amount of courage to carry out, but it can be a very effective negotiating technique.

3. *Manage concessions properly.* When you're using the GTS, don't make concessions unless they are minor ones. Once you've taken a hard stand on an issue, you can't back off at all without it being interpreted as a sign of weakness. Realistically your GTS has become "take it or leave it." If after you've adopted that stance the other side asks for some concessions and you give in, then you destroy your GTS. If the other side asks for something minor, you might concede the point, but even then you should appear to give in reluctantly. Let's say that as part of the discussion, you said you had to have their answer in two days. They come back and say, "Can you give us three days?" If the extra day is not critical, you can give in on this point because it doesn't effect the overall transaction. But you need to express reluctance even though the extra day doesn't really matter. So you may respond, "Yes, I'll give you the three days, but that's all. If you delay any longer, I'm history."

It is also important to accept concessions from the other side with hesitation. Once you have decided to use the GTS and you win a point, you should back up slowly. You may acknowledge a concession, for example, by saying, "Well, it's nowhere near what I wanted and even if we are making a little progress, we still have a long way to go."

4. *Aim high.* You will always come out better in the long run if you aim high in the beginning. This is good, basic goal-setting advice. It works in all situations, including negotiating by using the GTS. Whenever you make a statement about what you want, that will stick in the mind of your adversary. It becomes a starting point. In those rare instances when you get what you ask for it indicates that you started much too low. The other side needs the satisfaction of winning by giving you less than you asked for.

Remember, if you aim low and they accept your offer, you will not be satisfied with the outcome. You'll find yourself thinking, "They gave me what I wanted, but I probably would have gotten more if I aimed higher." For example, assume I am willing to sell my car for $25,000, but I tell you my price is $35,000. If I told you that $25,000 was the firm price I want and I won't accept less, you won't believe me and you'll still come back with a lower offer of maybe $22,000 or $23,000. At $35,000, I have left myself some room to negotiate and when I come down in my price you feel you've won something.

5. *Leave as much room as possible.* A successful negotiation depends on flexibility on both sides and also on your ability to move people off of their position. If you have only a narrow range of issues to discuss, that also narrows the possibilities for compromise. But the more issues you leave open, the more negotiating room you have to reduce your demands when it is to your benefit to do so. The more negotiation that occurs will bring you closer to goal you have set.

The example of my car makes this point. If you want to pay $20,000 and I ask $25,000, we are only $5,000 apart. When I ask for $35,000, I have created a much larger field for discussion. At the difference between $20,000 and $25,000, we only have room for a combined $5,000 of negotiation in one direction or the other. The *best* I could hope for would be to get the $25,000, and that is going to happen only if you cave in completely, which you will never be happy about. But when I say I want $35,000, I will appear to have made a major concession if I come down $8,000 to $27,000. Now I can say, "I met you more than halfway and $27,000 is an excellent price for a car like mine."

Let's say you play it cute and only raise your offer to $25,000. Guess what? Now I've gotten the price at which I was willing to sell, but I will still complain that I want more. If I had started out with a $25,000 price, you would never have agreed to pay it since you would have believed some further negotiation was possible. It is important to know that the initial price set by the seller should not be set so high that it scares away all bona-fide bidders. Likewise the offering bid by the buyer should not be so low that it's not treated by the seller as a serious bid.

6. *Don't succumb to the power of the simple solution.* A simple solution can be enticing. For example, you're negotiating a deal but both sides are far apart on the price. The seller wants $2.8 million and you only want to pay $2.4. So the seller says, "I'll tell you what. Why don't we just split the difference and make the deal at $2.6?"

That's a simple solution. But it may not be the right solution to the problem. For example, if your investigation leads you to believe that the building is worth a maximum of $2.5 million, why should you pay $2.6? Reaching an agreement is not the sole purpose of any negotiation. The deal has to be reasonable in the minds of both parties. So while the seller's proposed solution—splitting the difference—is simple and therefore has some compelling power behind it, it's not reasonable to you based on your information. . . .

You might come back to the seller by saying, "My investigation indicates the building isn't worth more than $2.3 million but I am willing to pay $2.4 million because I've spent too much time on this deal and it's time to finish it or kill it. We should be negotiating between the range of $2.3 million and $2.4 million, which is more realistic, but I'm willing to honor my $2.4 million dollar offer."

Now this is a GTS because you've rejected the seller's apparent compromise and resisted the power of the simple solution. You should adhere to the rule of "don't talk" as a guiding principle. You don't want to get into a discussion where you have to defend the nature or extent of your investigation.

Another simple solution that is often suggested is, "Let's resolve this by putting it up to one of the experts in the field to determine the fair price." The seller might want to bring in his own expert who he controls but the GTS compels you to shut off that avenue. You can resist this simple solution by saying, "I don't need some expert to tell me what I should pay for a piece of property. I'm willing rely on my own experience."

7. *Bargain small items for big ones.* Don't fall into the "staying even" trap. There does not have to be any tit for tat in a negotiation—certainly not when you've adopted a GTS. Yes, you might be willing to trade concessions with the other side, but the GTS dictates that you may bargain small points away in exchange for receiving big ones. However, your GTS does not lend itself to much more bargaining.

8. *Use deadlines to your advantage.* Experiments into various aspects of negotiation have shown over and over that deadlines are always a factor, and an important factor at that. They are the most effective way to get a decision made. As the deadline approaches, more deals get made.

When you are using the GTS, set a deadline that the other side will have difficulty meeting. You can use the difficult deadline as leverage to improve what you get in the deal.

Since you know that people have a natural desire to settle disagreements before deadlines arrive, the GTS increases the pressure.

9. *Be patient and stingy.* The other side always needs satisfaction. They want to come to an agreement. So the more patience you can bring to the table, the stronger your position. The patient negotiator has everything on his side: time, terms, details. This goes hand in

hand with being stingy. You can afford to be stingy with what you give up or demand, and the stingier you are the sweeter your concessions will taste when you finally give them up, no matter how small they really are.

It is very effective as a part of the GTS to take a hard line throughout the negotiations and then soften up toward the end when you sense that closure is at hand. The GTS in which you aren't willing to make any concessions at all takes great patience to stick to, so you must be patient *and* stingy to effectuate your closing strategy. Then when you soften up and begin making small concessions, the other side gets the sense that you're not so hard to deal with. They're winning. They feel that it's going to be a successful negotiation after all. Here is where you can concede all the little stuff while winning the points you think are vital. The patience and stinginess you used as part of your GTS will eventually pay off.

The other side needs, even *craves*, a sense of satisfaction from their negotiating performance. Even more, they need to know that something is going to get finished. Their desire for closure can cloud their judgment. As long as it doesn't cloud your judgment, you can use the desire for closure as an effective tool.

10. *Be careful in how you request a variation.* If you're a buyer, you have to establish the "standard" as an important starting point. If you plan to ask for any kind of a variation in the deal, you have to at least understand the basic standard itself. Otherwise, how can you measure the value of the variation?

For example, you need to get a brochure printed up. You visit the printer in his print shop and he tells me it will take three weeks to do the job. To set a standard, you have to know the price for getting 1,000 brochures in three weeks. I really want to get these brochures in 10 days. But in the absence of establishing the standard of what it normally costs for the three-week period, how can you evaluate the extra cost for doing the job faster?

So first you should ask for a quote for turnaround of three-weeks and he quotes you a price of $1,000. Now you can ask him, "Can you do it in 10 days?"

Of course he's going to say, "Yes, I can do it in 10 days but that costs extra."

Now that I know the price for three weeks *and* the price for 10 days, I am able to separate the two. I can evaluate the price difference by deciding whether it's worth the extra cost for the faster response time. If I'd started out saying, "I need this in 10 days," and if I failed to previously establish the cost of what is normal in terms of price and time, I can't quantify the cost of the variation against the benefits.

This can also serve as a starting point for further negotiation. You might have a lot of work coming up over the next year, so you can offer to give him all of your printing work if he will cut the typical turnaround time in half. You might agree to give him an exclusive if he promises you timely deliveries and gives you a price break in exchange for getting all of your work. If he refuses, your GTS tells you to say, "If you don't want the business on those terms, I'll find someone who does." None of this negotiation is possible until you know the *normal* cost and turnaround time, the value of the print shop's time constraints, and the negotiating power you can exert by promising an exclusive.

Even without promising an exclusive, you can still ask for the fast turnaround based on the premise that you are going to have a lot of work. So you ask for an introductory price break. The print shop wants that business, so even a meager incentive could get you a good deal.

Some people need more of a push than others. With them, the GTS often works like a charm.

13

DOS AND DON'TS OF
SKILLED NEGOTIATORS

Every skilled negotiator develops an innate ability to know what to do or what not to do in a situation. Donald Trump has this skill honed to a razor's edge.

In the 1970s, a mansion and estate in Palm Beach, Florida, went on the market—Mar-a-Lago. It was built in the 1920s by Marjorie Meriwether Post, heiress to the Post cereal fortune. This mansion had 118 rooms and 67 bathrooms and, overall, more than 67,000 square feet of floor space. The estate was spread out over 19 acres.

The trust that owned the property put it on the market at a high price. Donald Trump knew that the offer he was going to make was not going to be the high bid, but he thought he could get it anyhow if he gave them a compelling nonfinancial reason to sell it to him. Donald knew that the trust had given the estate to the State of Florida as a museum. For some unknown reason, it was not a popular attraction, and the state gave it back to the trust. The trust wanted to ensure that the mansion would be maintained as a national treasure. Knowing the trust's desires, Donald said, "If you sell it to me I pledge to keep the premises intact and to restore it to its original pristine condition." As part of the deal, Trump also offered to buy all of the furnishings.

This offer appealed to the trustees, who were attracted to the idea of a buyer maintaining the Post legacy. They sold the property and all its furnishings to Trump even though he was not the high bidder. True to his word, Trump refurbished the estate and restored it to its prior glory.

However, the taxes and the cost of maintenance were much too burdensome for a private residence. Trump thought, "Why shouldn't other people have the use of this masterpiece of elegance and workmanship?" Trump conceived the idea of turning the estate into a luxurious country club. Since many of the furnishings were valuable antiques of museum quality, he couldn't visualize having them abused by members, so he decided to sell the pieces at auction. The price they fetched was more than he paid for the entire estate when he bought it from the trust. But true to his word, Trump had all of the pieces of the original furniture replicated and replaced in their original locations. The local authorities didn't like the idea of a New Yorker with new money creating the most spectacular club in Palm Beach and refused to give him a permit to develop the country club. So Trump threatened to subdivide the 19 acres and build houses on it, which was permissible under the zoning rules. He knew the zoning officials hated the idea of more homes in the area and the loss of an historical treasure more then the idea of a country club and he exploited this knowledge until they finally relented.

With initiation fees in excess of $200,000 and $1,000-per-night rooming charges, Trump was able to make the exclusive country club concept extremely desirable to the moneyed families in the area. Belonging to Mar-a-Lago became synonymous with prestige. He created an aura of exclusivity and elegance that the wealthy in south Florida found extremely attractive.

In this negotiation for a challenging project, Trump exemplified many of the dos and don'ts that successful negotiators know so well. In this chapter, I provide you with eight important guidelines for becoming a skilled negotiator.

Do TRUST YOUR OWN INSTINCTS

Instincts guide us and protect us from repeating mistakes of the past. While you should make a habit of utilizing all available information, it's a mistake to ignore your instincts. When Trump negotiated with the Post trustees, he guessed correctly that they would be inclined to accept his lower offer because he promised to restore the prized jewel of the Post family to its original unique stature and maintain it as a national treasure. His instincts were right.

Generally speaking, everybody has developed a range of instincts over the course of their lives. Many are completely subconscious, but they are based on something we experienced. If the instinct is right, we accept it and operate based on it. If the instinct is wrong, experience dictates that we change it or discard it. The instincts you have developed are usually correct.

As an example, let's suppose that you and your spouse are walking down the street one night and at the end of the block you see a group of young, boisterous youths. Instinctively, you view this as a potentially dangerous situation. So you cross the street to avoid what your instincts tell you could be trouble. You'll take alternative action based on your past experience in the same or similar situations, or based on something you've heard or read.

When you meet someone in his office, your instincts—the sum of your experiences—help you to size up the person and to make a series of judgments about the kind of person you're dealing with. So if you're in a negotiation with someone and your instincts lead you to believe you can't trust him—without any specific basis for believing that—your instinct is probably right. You may have met with other people at various times with the same characteristics, using the same language, similar in any number of ways, and somehow your instincts force you to a conclusion. Someone might start out saying, "You can work with me because I'm an honest person." From your experience, you know that truly honest people don't have to tell you about their honesty, and that it's usually the *dishonest* people who make such claims. That's instinct.

My oldest brother was one of the greatest role models in my life, but not in the way you might think. During World War II, he was in an infantry division in the army and without the benefit of any formal education he rose through the ranks from private to lieutenant colonel. He had more citations for courage and bravery then he could wear on his chest. He was truly a respected leader of men. When my father died suddenly of a heart attack, I was only 16. With his untimely death, my hopes of becoming an engineer and graduating from MIT died as well. I can still vividly recall my brother saying to me, "George, don't worry at all. I'll pay for your entire college education when you're ready to go." Shortly thereafter, he was honorably discharged from the army and ready to conquer the business world.

His true character soon emerged. He was a super salesman in every sense of the word. He had grandiose ideas, but no money to turn them into reality. I think he could have sold sin to God. Everyone in the family was taken in by him at one time or another, and he hit them up for money they couldn't afford to lose. He formed a company called Teleon (the Greek word for perfection) and claimed he had the rights to the greatest steam iron ever invented. "No household will be without it," he said. He showed everyone a prototype that looked sensational and said he would let someone in on the ground floor if he or she gave him seed money for marketing. What he neglected to say was that he didn't have any production facilities and he really had no idea what the cost would be to market the product. He promised a 50 percent return on their investment in one year, and family and friends fell for it. He took the money, abandoned the steam iron idea, and instead decided to purchase huge amounts of foreign steel at a cheap price, but he never had the necessary financing to complete the deal. He always had the most expensive suits and cars and gave lavish gifts, but underneath he was just a con man.

I never forgot my brother who had the ability to convince people that black was white, but always chased the impossible dream instead of coping with reality. He eventually abandoned his wife and son and skipped town before his checks bounced and caught up with him. He disappeared and all the money he borrowed went with him; he never returned a dime to those who trusted him. Needless to say, he never paid a penny toward my college education.

The point of this story is that many times in my business life, I have found myself listening to someone talk and I would hear my brother talking. I'd say to myself, "This guy is a phony; he's a person who will promise the moon and the stars, but won't deliver. This guy is just like my brother Jerry." On each of those occasions, my instincts were always right. This can apply in all different aspects of negotiation, and not just with people. For example, if you're looking at real estate, you might dislike a particular place or building for no logical reason. However, as valid as your instincts are, they are only a starting point. You shouldn't take the position that you know you're right. But your instinct has triggered a reaction and you should exercise extreme caution.

Do Adopt Your Own Style of Negotiating

Donald Trump, always a visionary in his negotiations, brought his very personal style to the Mar-a-Lago negotiation. He did not deal strictly in the purchase price of the property, but also addressed the interests of the family and the trust. In his business style, imagination and vision play as important a role as the financing. Everybody has a basic character and style and that should always be the starting point for how you negotiate though you do need to adapt somewhat to fit the other person's style. If you try too hard to adopt or imitate somebody else's style, it comes out false. For example, if someone has a minimal education and he tries to mask it by using big words, it won't ring true. People will see through it every time. You should be true to yourself, your education, and your background. Use these genuine attributes to develop your negotiating style. It is important, however, to tailor your negotiating style to the particular circumstances that are evident in a transaction. If humor is appropriate, be humorous. If simple language is necessary to communicate with the other side, stay away from four-syllable words. If friendliness is the key, turn on the charm. Find a balance between being yourself and being like a chameleon that blends in with the environment.

DON'T TALK ABOUT YOUR WEAKNESSES

If you say too much to a good negotiator, he will seize on something you've said and use it against you. If you tell someone that the price is not an important thing to you, he is going to concentrate on a method that will enable him to get the highest price from you that he can. If you let him know you have no patience for drawn-out discussions, he is going to delay over and over to wear you down.

Trump went into the Mar-a-Lago negotiation without mentioning that he really didn't know what he would do with the property after he bought it. He also didn't apologize for making an offer that he knew was lower than other offers. He emphasized the strengths of his offer, namely his commitment to renovate the property and restore it to its former glory. He never mentioned or exposed any of his weaknesses.

The same rule applies to skill levels. If you tell the other side, "I'm not good at math," they're going to use some mathematical tactic such as overwhelming you with slanted numbers. If you tell the other person that you have a poor memory and can't remember details, he will believe he can slip things past you because of your tendency to forget.

Never talk about your weaknesses, but compensate for them. If you're not good at math, carry a pocket calculator. If you have a poor memory, keep meticulous notes. Don't hesitate to bring in experts to handle the areas in which you are weak. Accountants, attorneys, and note-takers can all help you to compensate for your shortcomings.

Do Coach Your Advisors to Say as Little as Possible

When you do bring a support staff into a negotiation, muzzle them. Don't let them speak for you unless you agree in advance on very specific statements they can make or you specifically ask them to answer a question of yours. It's important to realize that many deals are blown by non-negotiators. For example, if you're in the middle of a discussion and the seller states a price, you don't want your accountant to comment, "That price isn't a problem. We thought you'd ask for more." You don't want your allies to destroy a carefully mapped out strategy by saying the wrong thing. This applies to attorneys, accountants, investment advisors—anyone who can inadvertently give away information you don't want the other side to know. The accountant might think he's helping to make the deal happen, without realizing that he just swept the rug out from under your feet. You need to coach people you bring into the meeting, so that they help you cover up your weaknesses without diminishing your negotiating power.

Someone once came to negotiate a lease space in a building my client owned, and they brought a space designer along. I said to the designer, "Does our space fit your client's needs?" The space designer replied, "Your 12,000 feet provides the most efficient layout I've seen." This information was extremely important to me. Now I knew that my space had an efficiency that made it attractive to the other side. Telling me innocently enough what her opinion was increased my negotiating power. Her client should have coached her to not reveal information to me unless asked by the client to do so.

The opposite could also happen. For example, the space designer might have said, "We've been looking for 12,000 feet, but this is a poor space for us because it has a 30 percent loss factor." Now I would have information I didn't have before. I know the other side has focused on one of the drawbacks of my space. I recognize this defect and realize I will have to come up with some pluses to counterbalance that negative.

Don't Believe in the "Bogey" Theory

The bogey theory is often employed as a negotiating ploy. Someone trying to sell a house may say to you, "If that's your best offer, that's okay with me. I have two other offers that are better than yours, so I'll deal with them." If that were true, why are they even talking to you? Car salespeople use this ploy, too. They claim they have only one left in the model you like and someone else said he will buy it tomorrow. So you'd better make a decision right now if you want that car. This is meant to create interest through the illusion of scarcity and the pressure of time.

It's often not true. If, in fact, there were other people waiting in the wings, they wouldn't even bother to tell you. Why should they waste time on you, when someone else is standing in line just waiting to sign the papers? So the way to deal with this is to turn down the deal offered, but without slamming the door. You say, "Okay, if you have somebody else willing to give you a better deal, sell it to him. But if it falls through, give me a call, and if I'm still interested maybe we can meet again." By saying this, you create a delay so that you don't have to deal with the pressure. You defuse the bogey. But at the same time, be careful not to challenge the other side or call their credibility into question. You don't want to stop the other person from dealing with you in the future. You just tell them you're not willing to make a deal now.

When Trump was told by the zoning board in the Mar-a-Lago deal that they weren't going to let him turn the property into a country club because there were better uses for the property, he sensed that they were trying to bogey him. They thought they could get him to agree to any restrictions they wanted on the property just to get a permit, but Donald recognized what they were doing and he refused to play their game. Even though he had promised the Post family trustees that he was going to restore and preserve the property intact, he threatened the municipality by saying that if they didn't give him the country club permit, he'd tear down this priceless structure, subdivide the 19 acres, and build houses. Trump knew the governing powers of Palm Beach didn't want more housing on small lots. The zoning authority realized that he could legally do this under the zoning ordinances even if they amended them to thwart his efforts. Permitting Mar-a-Lago to become an exclusive country club operating under conditions they could live with was a better alternative, so ultimately they gave him the permits he needed. They didn't know that he would never break his word to the Post trustees. The authorities never knew that Trump's threat was a hollow one.

The basis for knowing a bogey claim is false can usually be found in the way it's expressed. If someone can make a better deal, he's not going to tell you about it, he'll make it. He would just show you the door and then call up the person with the better deal. There's no benefit in keeping you in the negotiation if he can do better elsewhere.

People keep using the bogey because it works so often. Many people believe that they have to agree to something (like buying a car) and they have to make the decision *today* because it's their last chance. The illusion has been created that if they walk away from this car at this price right now, they will lose the deal forever. If you think about it, how often have you heard about someone losing out on a good deal and not being able to find another one shortly thereafter?

Remember, when someone pulls a bogey on you and then does come back to you, that means something: Now you know you're the highest bidder and can lower your offer.

Don't Use All the Power You Possess

Relationships you establish during a negotiation are very rarely one-time relationships. There is a likelihood that you'll need to retain a good working relationship with one person or company, or even within an industry. You might be able to exert a lot of power to get what you want, but this doesn't mean it's wise to use all of your power in a single negotiation.

Clearly, if Trump believed he needed to be the high bidder on the Mar-a-Lago deal, he would have done so. He knew that he could stress the high cost of renovating the property, which had fallen into disrepair, to its prior glory. So he negotiated in a smart way to meet the desires of the trustees rather than offering a higher purchase price.

By leaving open the lengths to which you could go to make a deal happen, you can enter later negotiations with some new found steam in your arguments. By refusing to apply the maximum power you may possess, you can build your reputation. People will say of you, "He didn't push me to the wall. He's a nice person to deal with."

The give and take of negotiations is like stock. It can increase or decrease in value. You might need a good recommendation or reference from someone you're working with. For example, I once was dealing in a negotiation with a particular law firm that was representing a major lender in connection with a large loan on a prime office building on 5th Avenue in New York City. In choosing counsel to represent them, most lenders have an extensive list of law firms they will permit to represent them. As a matter of practice, the fees of the lender's lawyers are paid by the borrower. When a lender's law firm bills you for their fees, you have little choice but to pay those fees no matter how horrendous they may seem. There is an established range of reasonable fee levels in the industry, and most law firms will bill within that range. This particular law firm sent my client a bill far above the expected level. I thought it was unconscionable, and I told them so. I called up and said, "The amount of work you did on this transaction doesn't warrant a fee that high. I think a reduction is in order."

They replied, "That's our fee; it's nonnegotiable and that's what your client has to pay." The fee was paid, but I never forgave the law firm for their high-handed approach.

As a result, the next time I dealt with the same lender or another lender who wanted to use that law firm, I said specifically, "I won't deal with that law firm, pick someone else."

You can imagine how the lenders react when they hear this from two or three people. Guess what? That law firm gets dropped off the lender's list. With plenty of law firms on the list, the lender won't want to use attorneys that reputable attorneys representing major borrowers complain about. Negative comments can cause you to lose business without your ever knowing it and positive comments can bring you business from sources you were never aware of.

Don't Forget That There's No Right Price for the Wrong Item

If a transaction isn't satisfying in the broad sense, don't do it. For example, just because a product is made cheaply doesn't make it a *better* choice. If you have a retail store and you're shopping for space, you might have to pay three times more for a high-visibility spot with a lot of traffic than you would pay for a shop with no visibility and no traffic. You can boast to your friends that you got the space for one-third the price of what the other stores pay, but you're not going to be able to stay in business.

For example, what if Trump's analysis of Mar-a-Lago concluded that he could never be able to make the acquisition work financially? It would have been foolish to keep going just to win a trophy property. If there weren't enough benefits, he wouldn't have gone forward. As it turned out and as is often the case, he had many different ideas that could be implemented; his instincts told him when he started negotiations that this was going to be a deal he could make work.

Consider what happens when a man goes out to buy a car. The reason wives usually want to accompany their husbands is because they know what can happen. The husband's task was to find a good SUV in the $30,000 to $35,000 range so that his wife can run errands, take the kids to their sports practices, do shopping, and use it for family trips. So if she sends her husband off to buy an SUV and he comes home with a $54,900 Corvette two-seater sports car that he bought at a bargain price, she will have some choice words for him and they aren't, "That's nice dear."

It's the *wrong* car. Of course, he'll argue that it was a great price for that car, but his wife has the right to be furious. Right price, wrong item is all you need to remember.

Do Set Higher Goals within Realistic Limits

You have to define and create a *zone of uncertainty* concerning price or other key items that will be under discussion in a negotiation. By doing this, you identify what goals you initially ask for versus what you will accept. If you set high, but realistic goals, you establish one parameter of that zone. When Trump set his bid on the Mar-a-Lago project, he had to pick a number that was low enough to give him room to negotiate upward, but high enough to be taken seriously.

Instead of increasing his offer, he threw in the idea of renovation. Here's another example of how this *zone of* uncertainty works. If you're trying to sell your house for $350,000, you could offer it at $410,000, but you may have to justify the higher price on some logical basis such as condition, extra features, lot size, location, or view, for example. But there is always a realistic top price that no buyer will exceed for your type of house. That's the price you should initially ask. You know you'll probably get initial offers in the $300,000 to $320,000 range, but that's just the beginning. The zone of uncertainty has a top of $410,000 and a bottom of $300,000 to $320,000. Now that you know the boundaries, you negotiate to reach a mutually acceptable price within those boundaries.

This applies just as much to points other than price. If you're negotiating with someone and have to agree on a deadline, you know that as a general rule closing this type of deal should take three weeks. You may define the *zone of uncertainty* by saying you want a deal in 10 days. If the other side says, "I won't be able to get this done in less than three months," Now you know the parameters of this discussion and can work out an acceptable compromise.

When setting out your position, leave yourself as much room as you can to negotiate, but remember your position has to be perceived as a reasonable one by the other side. If they come to think that you're wasting time by making unreasonable demands, the negotiation will never get anywhere.

Every skilled negotiator can learn from the dos and don'ts in this chapter. I suggest that you memorize the guidelines I have set out and remember them throughout every negotiation. You will discover that they pay off in a big way when negotiations get difficult, or when people begin playing typical negotiation games. These rules help you maintain your perspective on what works and what doesn't, and on how to gain the upper hand in most negotiations.

14

TELEPHONE AND E-MAIL NEGOTIATION TIPS

THE TELEPHONE IS probably the most treacherous device ever created, at least for negotiations. It's not treacherous if you know how to use it, but most people do not. With cell phones, it's even worse. Disruptions to negotiations are deadly. Even without the telephone, it is all too easy to derail a discussion—unless of course, you don't like the way a negotiation is going and want to change the subject for a while.

Many years ago, I had a secretary, an Italian woman who was a stunning, olive-skinned beauty. Without even trying, she was the most sensual creature I'd ever seen. It wasn't her dress or makeup, nothing like that. It was the way she walked and talked; she radiated beauty and seduction. I was in an intense negotiation with four other lawyers. We were really going at it. I would have welcomed a change to the pace in the negotiation, but I didn't know how to do it without creating an incident. I needed a copy of a letter I had received so I phoned my secretary and asked her to bring that particular document to me. She brought it in and when she walked into the room, five lawyers looked at her and they all stopped talking. That was quite a feat. All she said was, "Here is the document you asked for, Mr. Ross." Then she simply walked out of the room. All five lawyers were stunned, and we all looked at each other and one of them asked, "What were we talking about?" The hostility in the room was instantly defused and from there on the negotiations went smoothly. That unplanned happening was so effective I made it a permanent part of my negotiating plans and used it many more times when the environment and the personalities warranted it. It never failed to achieve the desired result.

It's easy for someone to defuse a train of thought, to change the atmosphere of a negotiation with a little effort, so you must make a conscious effort to stay focused especially when distractions occur. It's hard enough to maintain focus in a face-to-face negotiation, but it's even worse when it is a telephone negotiation. It was many years before people were ready to accept telephones into their homes. They couldn't understand why anyone would want to put a device in his living room so that someone could summon him with a bell, any time he wanted, and start a conversation. Yet, this is what we have today, and existing technology has created an even more complex negotiating environment.

GOOD AND BAD ASPECTS OF THE TELEPHONE

The telephone acts as a speed-up device. It's very different from doing business in person. The time frame of a typical phone call versus a typical meeting effectively proves my point. Ask yourself, what would you consider a very long business call? One hour would be a very, very long business call. However, if you are negotiating in person, one hour is considered a short time to negotiate any meaningful transaction. For example, if you are buying a house, negotiations would take many hours of many days.

The very nature of the telephone forces everything to occur in a much shorter time frame than a face-to-face meeting. People are only capable of talking for a limited period and have a tendency to think, "Enough already; let's get it finished." This is a significant disadvantage because both sides end up with less information. Of course, once you know the pitfalls of a telephone negotiation, you can, with practice, use the telephone to your advantage.

Convenience

The convenience of the telephone is also its biggest drawback. If you're receiving a call, the timing could be hazardous to your negotiation strategy. If you're unprepared, distracted, or not in a negotiating mood, you can't control the timing of the incoming call. The person making the call immediately interferes with whatever you're doing at that time, the people you're with, and your schedule and that puts you at an immediate disadvantage. If you believe in the Golden Rule, "doing unto others what they do to you," the opposite works to your advantage. If you're the one making the call, then you are in control and it's up to the other side to realize the timing is not good and take some defensive action. It's ironic that as a rule people don't like to defer a phone call even when it's inconvenient. It would be so easy to say, "We have a time zone difference and I'm not awake yet. Can you call back in an hour?" But many people will say the timing is fine, even when it isn't. They willingly accept the disadvantage because they believe most calls are important. In our culture, we like to get things done quickly. We don't like putting off callers. So once a caller gets someone who's unprepared on the phone, the caller has a distinct advantage. The necessity to answer the telephone has been offset to a degree by caller identification and answering machines, but most people answer the phone when it rings.

SOME TELEPHONE TRAPS

Telephone calls often occur in chaotic situations. When you go into a face-to-face meeting, you will have prepared a thorough outline of goals, a comprehensive list of agenda items, a stack of research kits ready to pass out, and you will have assembled all of the support staff you need to make a compelling argument. Using the telephone, you cannot be as well prepared. The agenda is about the only item that can be adapted to a telephone negotiation. If you're making the call, it's almost a certainty that the other side isn't well prepared. The big question for every telephone negotiation is, "How important is the item that one side or both is going to forget?"

Here are a few suggestions that will give you a huge advantage in any telephone negotiation: Before you make a call, prepare a written agenda for yourself. List, in priority, the points you want to cover and make sure you cover them all. Whenever someone initiates the call to you, ask him exactly what he wants to talk about, and just listen and make notes of what he is saying. This should be a one-way conversation—he talks and you listen. It's okay to ask for some clarification and to add, "I got it" from time to time, but any meaningful discussion is not started. At the end of the call, you simply say, "You caught me at a bad time right now. I'm in the middle of something, so I'll call you back."

You can take 10 minutes, an hour, a day, whatever you need to be able to respond in a well-conceived, intelligent fashion to the items that were raised in the earlier call. Then, when you call back, you're in the driver's seat. Now you know exactly what you plan to say, but the other side is not adequately prepared to respond to your thoughts.

Remember, people have a tendency to forget things during telephone meetings. So let the other side ramble on in the normal, informal manner of most telephone discussions and, as I said before, just listen. Someone will, indeed, forget something, and it is most often the person who receives the call and elects to respond without giving careful consideration to the consequences. That receiver is far less likely to be prepared; the person making the call is better prepared, even if it's only an informal mental list of things he wants to discuss. As with all negotiations, the telephone negotiation is going to be dominated by the more organized side. You have to train yourself to always be prepared in any telephone negotiation, and train yourself to be ready for every negotiation, especially the ones you have by telephone. You should have at your fingertips all documents you may need, an agenda of items to be discussed, a calculator, an estimate of the duration of the call, and anything or anyone pertinent to the discussion. Don't forget the words of Louis Pasteur: "Chance favors the trained mind."

There's No Face-to-Face

One of the biggest flaws in a telephone negotiation is that you can't react to anything but the other person's voice. You don't see any facial expressions, any body language, or interplay with others on the call or any of the many forms of input we might ordinarily use to judge the effect of our message on others—or to gauge the conviction the other side has for the arguments they make.

If you want to get a "no," use the telephone. It's the worst forum for making a convincing argument and for changing someone's mind. The reactions of other people are invisible to you, so it's much easier for anyone to play power games with you without you even being aware of it. For example, if you're in a conference call and you make a statement, one person on the other side can convey thoughts to the other person with a facial expression or gesture that you will never see. That won't work in a live, face-to-face negotiation. The lack of input in a live and in-person discussion is a huge handicap, especially if you are alone and there are two or more people on the other end of the line.

You Never Know Who Is Listening

The telephone negotiation presents a special type of challenge. You never really know who is on the other end and what their roles are. The other side might not tell you the truth even if you ask. They might say, "It's just me on the line today," and you might answer, "Good. I'm glad John Smith isn't listening because I can't talk to that SOB since he only creates problems but never comes up with a solution."

And, of course, John Smith is on the phone and now he's a worse enemy than he was before.

If you were in a room face-to-face, you can see who is there. Or the other side might tell you, "Just between you and me, my accounting people don't like your numbers." You can defend your numbers easily enough and you might even be inclined to say something derogatory about accountants in general. But the CFO or some other accountant may also be on the phone. They may be scribbling notes to the person you're talking to, telling him what to say, what to ask, and how to answer. This puts you at a tremendous disadvantage because you don't realize who's there and who is controlling the negotiation.

You have to play defense on the telephone. Assume someone else *is* listening in to your conversation and that you have to be careful about what you say. If you believe that you suffer any disadvantage in a telephone discussion, insist on a face-to-face meeting.

This disadvantage can be applied in reverse, of course. If you're going to have a telephone negotiation with someone, you might be wise to have *your* accountant (or lawyer, president, or other advisor) there scribbling notes to you, telling you what to say. If there is going to be an advantage and a disadvantage, you're better off having the former than suffering from the latter.

Interruptions Are Deadly

Negotiations always have a certain momentum at a particular time. Every interruption to the normal flow is a setback. No person can maintain his focus or posture while interruptions are occurring. If you are interrupted, your mind goes elsewhere and your train of thought is destroyed; and the more interruptions there are, the worse this becomes. So if you're on the telephone with someone and he keeps excusing himself to talk to someone else who came into the room or called on another line, you have to nip it in the bud. You need to say, "Call me at a time when you can talk without interruptions. How's 3:00 P.M. today? Block out 45 minutes and call me then."

Ironically, when you're on the telephone, you might have the habit of accepting the kinds of interruptions that would be entirely unacceptable if you were in a live meeting. Someone else in your office would never think of disrupting a meeting by walking into the room and asking you a question; but he can telephone you and if you take the call, they have achieved the same result. Sometimes interruptions occur that must take precedence over any telephone negotiation. For example, if Donald Trump walks into my office while I'm in the middle of a telephone call, there's no way I can concentrate on that call while Donald's waiting. I immediately tell the listener, "Something came up that requires my immediate attention, so I'll have to call you back." Notice I didn't say when I would call; so the timing is all mine if Donald's visit requires some immediate action.

You Can't Examine Documents

If you're in a face-to-face negotiation, you can make the argument, "I've got figures right here that justify my position." You can present the proof to the other person as you're talking. You can't do that on the telephone.

Have you ever been on the phone and heard the other person rustling papers? He's looking for the document that justifies his position, but what good is it? All you hear is the rustling of paper. You can't see it. Just as you can't read the other person, you also can't read the other side's documents and they can't read yours.

Both sides are at a disadvantage in this situation. One side can't refute the other side's points because they don't see the other side's documents. You really don't even know if they have any compelling evidence. It could be a negotiating ploy when on the telephone to claim to have compelling evidence, knowing the other side can't demand to see it right then and there. So the other person tells you during a real estate negotiation, "I have a survey by a reputable brokerage firm showing that the average rent for a building such as yours is only $28 per square foot." You're asking for $35. How do you refute the other side's survey when you're negotiating on the phone? The survey might not exist. It might be five years old. It might have been the result of poor sampling. You have no way of knowing that if you can't examine the document.

There Is a Tendency to Expect Resolution

This is a trap that is indigenous to a telephone negotiation. Somehow, on a telephone call, people expect some type of agreement to result. That doesn't always happen in a face-to-face meeting.

In a face-to-face negotiation, you may come to the point where you want to say, "Let me think about this for a couple of days, and then we can get back together." That's not unusual when you're there with the other person. But on the telephone, both parties are prone to settle something, one way or the other. If we talk about some issue for 15 or 20 minutes, we both think we have the right to get a definitive answer then and there.

LEARNING TO MASTER THE TELEPHONE

Now that we've given some thought to the intricacies of telephone negotiations, I'm going to show you how to become a master at turning telephone negotiations in your favor.

Learn to Listen

People don't listen intently on the phone. That's the main thing for you to remember. The basic reason for slipshod listening is that you don't know when something important is coming, only after it has been said. At the same time, you don't really know if the other party is really listening to you, so the problem is twofold. Without any visual cues, you're only responding to what you hear, so you need to put extra effort into really listening intently to what the other side is saying and making notes to remember some key items.

If you want to drive somebody crazy in a telephone negotiation, don't say anything for a few minutes. Before long the other side will get frantic and say, "Are you still there? Did we get disconnected? Can you hear me all right?" or something akin to that. In a face-to-face meeting, there are numerous situations where either one or both sides are silent, maybe just contemplating an answer. On the telephone, the lack of talking indicates a complete breakdown of communication, so the last speaker feels compelled to fill the void. When you let this happen, the other side is compelled to do the talking and you will learn a lot more about them than they can learn from your silence. In some situations, this will result in the other side giving you much more than they ever would if you were in a room with them.

Ask the Purpose of the Call

Any time someone calls you, always ask what his agenda is—why he is calling. Then just listen carefully to his response and talk only when there is more information you can obtain by your response. If he says, "I think the price you're asking is too high." You may respond by asking, "What do you think is the right price?" You're getting more information, but you haven't agreed that the price is too high, and you haven't even indicated that you're willing to negotiate. But if he gives you an alternative price, at least you know what his thinking is. You have gained information while giving none in response.

After getting all of the information you can, you still want to be in control of the agenda. So you should say, "Let me consider what you've said and I'll get back to you." If it's to your advantage, you can set a time for you to continue the discussion, otherwise just leave the time open. Meanwhile, you can take whatever action you think is appropriate to tailor a response. Then when you call him back, you are prepared and have supporting information to bolster your position. You already know how much he said he is willing to pay. You also know at what price you would be willing to sell. If the range of uncertainty is narrow, it should be relatively easy to bridge the gap. Maybe, "Let's split the difference" might be the way to go, or some other appeal to human nature that we discussed earlier. If the gap is wide, you will need to present some compelling reasons for the other side to revise their numbers or prepare to abort with a "take it or leave it" stance.

Always Use a Checklist or Agenda

You should get in the habit of creating and updating a telephone checklist or phone call agenda that lists items in priority order to ensure that you won't leave anything out. You want to be sure to gather as much information as possible if the other side initiates the call, so that when you call them back, you're prepared for everything. So when you're done discussing price and you know what number they have in mind, you can ask, "What else do you want to talk about?" Maybe delivery dates, representations, or other issues will be raised.

When you call back, you have your checklist and agenda and the arguments you will use with whatever backup you need. Then you will be as organized and prepared as you can possibly be.

Don't Hold Telephone Negotiations Where Interruptions May Occur

You want to be sure you won't be interrupted during an important telephone negotiation. You should close your door and alert a receptionist or secretary not to put through any calls until you say so. You can control this on your side, but you won't be able to control the same thing for the other side unless you insist on it as a condition for your call. You can say, "We have a lot to discuss and we should do it without interruptions. I can clear an hour at 9 A.M. tomorrow. Is that okay with you?" Pick a time that works for both parties, and you'll be surprised how much will be accomplished. One excellent way to avoid interruptions is to create what I call "a quiet hour." Set aside an hour in which you will make all the calls you need to make, but will not permit any outside interruptions (i.e., personal visits, deliveries, or in-coming calls). I have found that my quiet hour is the equivalent of at least 80 minutes. Try it for yourself and you'll be amazed at how much you can do in that hour.

Have All Materials Available When on the Phone

If there is a lot of documentation involved with your negotiation, the telephone is the worst venue to use. But if you have to talk on the phone, be well organized and have everything ready. Have all of your documents easily accessible and well organized to make your arguments.

You would never talk into a face-to-face meeting without organizing your materials. Many people are so casual about telephone negotiations that they are ill-prepared to negotiate intelligently. Knowing this puts you in control. If you organize well and prepare everything, you will have a clear advantage.

It's not just your materials that should be well prepared. You should be sure you have anticipated all that you may need. For example, be prepared to crunch numbers if necessary. Most negotiations involve money and a discussion of it, so you have to be ready to do some on-the-spot number crunching. If numbers may be involved, be sure you have a calculator handy and you or someone on your side knows how to operate it.

Take Good Notes

You might be a great note-taker in face-to-face meetings, but in a telephone negotiation, I cannot stress enough the importance of good note taking. You must take good notes about all phases of the discussion—what was decided, areas of continuing disagreement, definition of the issues, and itemization of new issues. To be of any value to you, your notes must be *immediately* filed when the call is over. If you wait and the notes get lost or misplaced, you would be better off if the telephone call never took place. Most negotiations consist of a series of discussions and meetings. So your notes should be dated; list the name of person or persons on the other side, and they should be detailed. You should assume you will need to refer to them again later and if you are sloppy, you will pay the price for it.

Most people don't take the kind of notes I'm referring to. If you have ever watched someone while they're on the phone, they might be having an intense negotiation, talking about important issues, but not taking a single note and maybe even doodling. The telephone negotiation counts as much as a face-to-face meeting, but without notes it is much more difficult to pin down the other side. If the other side doesn't recall the details of a discussion, it is powerful to be able to tell them the time and date of the conversation, and read back what they said. If they don't have good notes, you'll win that argument hands down.

Confirm the Conversation with a Follow-Up Letter

I've talked previously about documenting your meetings with a periodic follow-up letter summarizing the issues: what was decided, what remains, deadlines, and so on. But this is even more important after a telephone negotiation because people are so casual about telephone conversations they have a tendency to forget what was said. They are prone to forget the details of their agreements, and they have a tendency to take the telephone negotiation less seriously. Documenting the details of a telephone negotiation is more critical than it is with a face-to-face meeting.

People will very rarely respond to the letter by saying, "That's not we agreed on" or "That's not what we discussed." They either don't read your letter or e-mail or they don't think the issues you stated are important enough to take issue with immediately. Here again, people underestimate the importance of a telephone negotiation, so they are not likely to challenge anything you say in a follow-up letter. The follow-up letter or e-mail becomes a very important document later if the other side contradicts or conveniently forgets something they agreed to in a previous telephone negotiation.

E-Mail Rules of Thumb

Unlike the telephone, e-mail communication leaves a paper trail. So the odds are better that everyone will at least take seriously what they write down.

Some important things to remember about e-mail:

- *Grammar and punctuation make impressions.* There is a tendency for people to not check spelling in e-mail, but they should. Spelling and punctuation are not just old-fashioned ideas; they create an impression about your education and intelligence and your attention to detail. They also convey the idea that you care about the impression you make on other people.
- *Nonverbal expressions can be misinterpreted, so be careful.* When you have only the words to read, you can't hear the tone of voice. So if I write to you, "It's important that we discuss this immediately," you can't tell whether I'm in a friendly mood or angry

with you. You don't know if I'm being casual or demanding. So I have to be careful how I construct my message.

For example, I might write to you, "As you and I have already discussed, the document has to be recorded by tomorrow to meet our contractual deadline. It's important that we discuss this immediately." Now, with an explanation preceding my previous statement, it makes more sense. I'm providing an explanation so you will respond more readily.

I received an e-mail from a woman not long ago. We'd been exchanging e-mails and working out some details to a deal. All that the message said was "No thank you."

The lack of tone can be easily misunderstood, or even be thought to mean something completely unintended. This concerned me because things had been going along quite well, so I was puzzled and, frankly, I couldn't remember exactly what I'd said in my last e-mail. So I looked it up. She had sent me several things I had requested and I'd sent a reply that simply said, "I received your information. Thank you."

Now her e-mail made sense. She had meant to answer my "thank you message" by saying, "No. Thank *you*" (i.e., she was thanking me for something I had done for her earlier). But her tone of gratitude didn't come through. That, combined with a lack of grammar and emphasis, could have led to a misunderstanding.

- *Follow-up is important and courteous.* Following up after a complicated discussion is an effective negotiating tool and a courtesy. Whether your meeting took place in person, by telephone, or by e-mail, a summary is always a smart idea. You can start out by saying, "Thank you for all of your hard work in resolving the details. I'm sure we will be able to arrive at a solution to the remaining issues." You then summarize what you've agreed on, what else needs to be done, and what deadlines, if any, have been set.

This maintains clarity and perspective during the negotiation. It also keeps communication open and avoids misunderstandings. E-mail is an easy method because it doesn't take up any office space. The other side can move your e-mail to an online folder without needing physical file space and retrieve it easily later on.

As long as you are keenly aware of the problems in telephone and e-mail communication, you should be able to manage problems as they arise—and manage them so that they do not handicap you during your negotiations. Being aware of the pitfalls makes you a better negotiator.

Notice that I never used the words, "telephone conversation" in this entire chapter but rather "telephone negotiation." Every telephone call or telephone conversation, no matter how casual, is in fact a negotiation and you should give it as much importance as any other type of negotiation. Don't forget it.

15

When to Use Nonbinding Letters of Intent or Memoranda of Understanding

A BINDING COMMITMENT you might obtain from other people is not limited to a signature on a contract. Every negotiation—especially a Trump-style negotiation—is based on developing a personal relationship with other people and deriving the benefits that grow from it. These include something beyond the legalities of a contract. A *moral* commitment from a person who is trustworthy is often better and stronger than a legal one. I can personally attest that this trait runs in the Trump family.

When Donald Trump was working on Trump Tower, he needed access to Walter Hoving, the CEO of Tiffany & Co. He wanted to negotiate for the purchase of Tiffany's excess air rights at their 5th Avenue location and a purchase of their option on the Kandell property next to Trump Tower. Donald's father and Walter Hoving had done some business together and Donald's father suggested to Donald that he could work out a fair deal with Hoving in a short period of time. A meeting was set up in Hoving's office with Hoving, a young attorney from Coudert Brothers who was counsel to Tiffany, Fred Trump, and me. There had been prior discussions between Fred Trump and Walter Hoving that were to be finalized at that meeting. Fred and Walter shook hands on the deal and we were about to leave when the attorney from Coudert said he had prepared a document for Fred Trump to sign. Hoving asked to see the document, looked it over, and proceeded to tear it up. Looking at his attorney, Hoving said, "Young man, you may be a good lawyer, but you have a lot to learn about dealing with people. When Fred Trump makes a deal, his word is good enough and there's no need for a written document."

This doesn't mean you can do away with documents. In a complex negotiation, the working documents you prepare can serve to define the issues and bring the entire transaction into focus and create that all-important moral commitment for which Trump-style negotiating is known. Good working documents add to the time investment by both parties, which helps build commitment to the deal. And they help to save time and disagreements later by serving as an outline for those final, legal documents.

Trump's World Tower at the United Nations is a perfect example of the way good documents in a negotiation can support key verbal agreements. Building this project was not a simple matter of buying the land and getting permits. Trump wanted to build the tallest residential structure in New York, and to do this he needed to acquire air rights, which allow a developer to build a taller building than he otherwise could. Under New York laws, you are allowed to transfer air rights from one property to another on the same block. So to develop a very tall building, Trump needed to buy air rights from adjoining landowners. This was complicated because he had to negotiate with many people at the same time and keep it all confidential as well. If word of what he was trying to do became public, the price of the air rights would have immediately skyrocketed. He proceeded to make verbal deals with all the owners in which he promised them the highest price that he offered to any one of them. Their reliance on his word enabled him to make deals with everyone before word spread about his intentions. As you might imagine, all of these arrangements, promises, contracts, and purchases of rights involved a lot of written documents, even before the deal got to its stage of execution of legal and binding documentation. But the verbal agreement was never violated.

The Value of a Nonbinding Letter of Intent or Memorandum of Understanding

To bring a transaction into focus, especially a complex one, you must begin with a thorough and clear definition phase to crystallize the thinking of the parties. This is where a *letter of intent* (LOI) or a *memorandum of understanding* (MOU) can be very helpful. The deal can initially be discussed in general terms, but to clarify the understanding of all parties you may need to prepare and distribute a piece of paper with the whole deal summarized. There is little practical difference between an LOI and an MOU, both of which should be nonbinding to achieve the desired result—a review without involving lawyers. The LOI is usually used to outline a transaction before too much discussion has occurred. The MOU is typically utilized after the parties have met and agreed on several items. The purposes of an LOI or MOU are identical, so don't sweat the label. Each LOI or MOU should be very brief, a page or two at most, with very concise language. It summarizes the *intentions* of both sides. The LOI or MOU should specifically state that it is not a legal document that when signed is binding on either party. In light of this, it shouldn't read like it was prepared by a lawyer. It should be more informal in tone, and much shorter and less detailed than the actual contract that is prepared later by your legal counsel. It should hit the highlights of the deal in general terms with a minimal amount of specificity. It's like an artist's sketch on canvas outlining the picture, before he begins applying paint. He sketches in the outline of what he is going to paint and what it will look like, but the actual details are to be added later.

The LOI or MOU Engenders Better Thinking

In the course of preparing an LOI or MOU, you not only focus on what you have agreed on, but also on what has not yet been agreed on.

Since it can double as a type of interim negotiation status report, the LOI or MOU can do much to bring both parties to the same level of understanding even though there has not been a complete meeting of the minds.

For example, let's say you write in the LOI or MOU that "the purchase price for the property is $500,000." But many aspects of the deal have yet to be clarified. When is it to be paid? How much of a down payment is required? Are there any contingencies? The purchase price is just a starting point. The LOI or MOU stimulates thought on both sides as to what has been negotiated and what remains to be negotiated.

Highlights Terms That Were Not Negotiated

It is often just as important to clarify terms that might not have been raised or fully discussed. These might not be obvious to both sides, or one side might have an entirely different take on the agreement than the other side. As you go through your preparation of an LOI or MOU, details arise that you realize weren't discussed. Once you recognize that fact, you prepare a list of the issues not yet discussed and create a new agenda for their negotiation.

Fills the Gaps in Continuity

In most negotiations, differences arise between the two sides because there is a break in the continuity of the negotiation. As long as both sides continue talking, they can resolve the areas where different positions have surfaced. The longer the time gap between negotiating sessions, the greater the likelihood that memories will get hazy. So when a negotiation stops, the LOI or MOU serves as a bridge, to indicate what has been agreed on or not agreed on as of its date.

Negotiation often consists of hundreds of smaller negotiations. I call this the "theory of transactional fractionalization." The negotiation is actually a series of individual negotiations that take place at different times, under different circumstances, and with different parties involved. Ultimately, all of these individual negotiations are blended into the final completion of the deal. Because there is usually some kind of time lapse involved between start and finish, this multitude of smaller negotiations can cause problems because both sides are likely to forget exactly what was discussed, when it was discussed, and if a final resolution has been reached. An LOI or MOU summarizes the multitude of smaller agreements that both sides have reached and shows the amount of progress the parties have made toward a final settlement. If you have excellent notes or a play book, it will be an easy task for you to summarize the state of negotiations at any time.

WHO CONTROLS THE DOCUMENT?

Whenever you draw up an LOI or an MOU, recognize the power you gain by putting your thoughts down on paper. It defines the agreement; it provides a chance for the other side to agree or to disagree; and in the absence of a response, your tacit agreement on its contents will make it easier to finish the deal.

Two aspects of an LOI or MOU are worth noting:

1. *Document control is important.* Whenever you have the chance to draw up documents, you should take it. This refers to contracts, amendments, leases, and, of course, any LOIs or MOUs. The person preparing the document decides what goes in, what gets emphasized, and what gets left out.

    You know what you want to draw attention to, and you also know what you choose to leave out because of its controversial nature. The other side will read what you put in the LOI or MOU, but they will have to figure out for themselves what you left out. Not only is it true that most people are poor note keepers and fail to follow up communications in a timely manner, they are often blinded by your written words and conclude that you have accurately summarized the whole deal.

2. *The LOI or MOU may reveal the hidden negotiators.* You sometimes get the sense in a negotiation that the person you're talking to is operating under a set of restrictive guidelines and doesn't actually make the final decisions. When you send out a nonbinding LOI or MOU and request a signature indicating approval, pay attention to who signs or initials it when it comes back.

The person signing the LOI or MOU may be the actual decision maker. If it is initialed by the other side's attorney or legal department, then you know it went through a legal review. If the CFO signs off, then it was scrutinized from a financial point of view. If someone else who you never met signs the LOI or MOU, like the CEO of the company, you know that he or she is the real power behind the negotiation on the other side.

Getting approval of your LOI or MOU is a powerful, important step. You need to know who has to agree on the LOI or MOU. Understanding the scope and knowing the people participating in the approval process makes it hard for anyone on the other side who has signed off on the document to raise new issues at a later date.

A Guide for the Legal Documents

The structure of an LOI or MOU should be viewed as a preliminary draft of what will ultimately become a legal agreement. That way, an attorney can't simply go off and make up a contract without making it conform to the agreements as defined and described in the LOI or MOU. It prevents someone from making last-minute changes to items that have been agreed on. While a legal contract can certainly embellish on the terms set forth in the LOI or MOU, it cannot change the contents or what the other side agreed to, either explicitly or implicitly.

CREATES A *MORAL* COMMITMENT AND ADDS TO TIME INVESTED

Some aspects of every negotiation are intangible. The LOI or MOU helps clarify and define these important, but intangible, issues for both sides. As you draft the LOI or MOU, you may discover that these issues are clarified in your mind, simply as a part of the process of articulating your point of view. Just because something is intangible doesn't mean it is not important.

Moral Commitment Is Sometimes More Important Than Legal Commitment

Very often, an LOI or MOU—even though both expressly state that they are nonbinding—may actually create a moral commitment that both sides feel obligated to honor. It may be an agreement to negotiate in good faith, for example. The agreement may even be unspoken. The LOI or MOU may transform an intangible into a tangible.

If the other side agrees with what you write in your LOI or MOU, and feels morally committed, he will be reluctant to come back later and contradict that agreement. The act of seeing the LOI or MOU and acknowledging its acceptance is powerful. For someone to disagree, he has to take specific steps to discuss the disagreement by communicating with you. If he doesn't communicate with you, then you have a moral commitment from him that is only good to the extent of his morality.

I tell people that this is often more valuable than a legal commitment. This is even more binding if approval is obtained from a key executive or board of directors. The LOI or MOU is also valuable because it gets you beyond the phase where one side is asking, "Should we make a deal or not?" Once you define the essence of the deal in the LOI or MOU, it articulates the deal in a way you believe the agreement exists. That makes it easier for the other side to agree since the LOI or MOU serves as a map of the deal.

Time Investment Is Important to Negotiators

The time investment—the importance of time put into the negotiation—is important to both sides and the negotiation itself gains value. The LOI or MOU are yet another step adding to the time investment. If you prepare the LOI or MOI, that takes up your time. When the other side receives it, they spend time reading it and discussing the deal. There may be more time spent if they want to modify the LOI or MOU and send it back to you, and then you also spend more time reviewing it. So both sides increase their invested time, and that motivates them to make the deal succeed.

16

THE MOST INTRICATE
DEAL I EVER NEGOTIATED

O CCASIONALLY, YOU MAY come across a transaction where a participant refuses to negotiate because he feels that his position is so strong he can control the outcome just by playing hardball. Or a key player may be absent, making a transaction very difficult to complete. But it can be done—it just takes a little extra tenacity and creativity. I remember a deal just like that with the Katz Agency. Although it was not a Trump deal, it had all the earmarks of a Trump-style negotiation. As I go through the scenario, I will identify factors, terms, and techniques (in parentheses) that have been discussed in this book, so you can see how these things played out in a complex high-stakes negotiation. Since the transaction was so dramatic, I have written it like a play—in three acts.[1]

ACT 1

Background

All of the action takes place in New York City in 1990. A major recession has been in progress and companies have shelved any expansion plans they had. Many prominent builders recently built buildings on speculation—without any commitments from tenants—believing that the rental market would recover by the time their buildings were completed. That didn't happen and as a result there was an over abundance of vacant space with no takers. At that time, the Katz Agency (now the

---

[1] The characters are real but the square footages and dollar amounts are fictitious.

Katz Media Corporation), which was a titan in the sale of radio and TV time to advertisers, was contemplating a merger that would substantially increase its space needs by at least 50,000 square feet. Katz was headquartered in 150,000 square feet of space at 1 Dag Hammarskjöld Plaza on 2nd Avenue, in a 750,000 square foot building between 47th and 48th Streets. This sounds like a lot of technical detail but you'll see why it's important to the story in a minute.

About half of the Katz Agency's space was covered by one lease (I'll call it the "Good Lease"). The rest of the space had been leased at various times as the need arose and was subject to several separate leases (the "Bad Leases"). The Good Lease covered about 75,000 square feet of space and had a remaining term of approximately three years. The rent for the Good Lease space was $25 per square foot, which was cheap by the standard of the time. My task was to renegotiate the Good Lease and the Bad Leases and get Katz the additional space it needed for the merger, while also taking advantage of the depressed real estate market.

Cast of Characters

GEORGE H. ROSS ("ROSS"): A consultant for the Edward S. Gordon Company ("ESG") a reputable real estate brokerage firm in New York. Ross is an experienced negotiator and real estate attorney who was hired as the chief negotiator for Katz.

LARRY RUBEN ("RUBEN"): Katz's current landlord, a respected and smart real estate developer who owned 1 Dag Plaza. Ross and Ruben had done many deals in the past and had mutual respect for one another (*a relationship*). Ross knew that Ruben was a tough negotiator who would exercise as much power as he had (this was *actual knowledge* proven by experience—not *apparent knowledge*). Ruben believed that Ross knew the business of real estate and had a reputation as a deal maker, not a deal breaker (*actual knowledge*).

JIM GREENWALD ("GREENWALD"): The head honcho of the Katz Agency and a close friend of Ross (*relationship*), as well as an investor in Beck-Ross Communications Corp., a Ross-owned entity that owned and operated several radio stations.

HARRY MACKLOWE ("MACKLOWE"): A respected, smart developer who in 1988 had built a major office building at 125 West 55th Street in New York City. The building was completed more than a year before this negotiation, but was still completely vacant, so Macklowe was in trouble. Ross and Macklowe had done deals in the past, had an amicable working relationship (*building trust*), and they knew they were both deal makers (*actual knowledge*).

Scene 1

Place: After reviewing and analyzing the Good Lease and the Bad Leases (*obtaining critical information necessary to formulate a strategy*), Ross meets Greenwald for lunch (*creating a friendly environment*).

ROSS: "Jim, tell me exactly what you would like me to accomplish for you" (*finding the story*).

JIM: "George, I'm in serious negotiations to complete a merger for $20 million that will strengthen Katz's position in the market. I have some lousy leases at 1 Dag that are all over the place regarding expiration dates and rents. I would like to consolidate my entire operation and make a new deal with Ruben that will handle my expanded space needs and get me a rent I can afford. Can you help me?"

ROSS: "Sure, Jim. I know Ruben well, so I'll arrange a meeting with him to test the waters and I'll tell you what happens."

Ross goes back to his office and prepares for his meeting with Ruben using the *POST technique* (described in Chapter 9) for the initial negotiation:

P = Persons. Ruben and Ross will meet at Ruben's office. Ruben will probably have his son there to hear what Ross has to say.

O = Objective. To see if Ruben is amenable to recasting the Good Lease and the Bad Leases and leasing more space to Katz.

S = Strategy. To try to convince Ruben that this approach eliminates the uncertainty of the rental market in three years when the Good Lease expires, and affords him the benefit of Katz occupying more space.

T = Tactics. Tell Ruben about the distinct possibility of Katz vacating Ruben's building entirely and making a deal for space in a new vacant building on Manhattan's West Side (*creating a bogey*).

Ross prepares a checklist of items to be discussed at the meeting:

1. Does Ruben have an additional 50,000 square feet available to lease to Katz?
2. Is Ruben happy with Katz as a tenant?
3. How amenable is Ruben to recasting the Katz leases?

Scene 2

Place: Ruben's office sometime later. Ross, Larry Ruben, and Ruben's son are present.

ROSS: "Larry, I've been engaged by Katz to solve their space problems in your building. They would like to take more space. Right now only one of their leases is at a rent consistent with today's weak market."

RUBEN: "George, Katz is a good tenant; they pay their rent on time and I would be interested in making a new lease for more space and renegotiating the Good Lease but I won't touch the Bad Leases. I like the high rents and the staggered expirations. That's my position" (*take it or leave it*). "You know that if I want to I can beat any deal you make elsewhere so it's best to deal with me."

ROSS: "Then I'll have to make a deal on a new vacant building on the west side where the owners are dying for a tenant like Katz and see if you can beat that" (*creating a bogey*).

RUBEN: "Come on, George we both know that the rents on those new buildings have to be high to satisfy the mortgagees. You also know that Katz's remaining obligation on the leases in my building is several million dollars. No builder in his right mind will take over that obligation. Katz's only hope is to make a deal with me. No one can make a better deal then I can. Plus Katz will save the cost of moving, creating a new installation, and an untold amount of aggravation. I hold all the cards (*intimidation*). Come back to me with a reasonable proposal and I'll consider it."

Scene 3

Place: Jim Greenwald's office. Ross and Greenwald are present.

ROSS: "Jim, I met with Ruben and any deal with him will be tough to swallow because he knows that if he wants to he can beat any deal you make elsewhere. I've examined your leases and you've got real troubles with the high rents and long terms on a lot of your space."

GREENWALD: "What can we do?"

ROSS: "I've got an idea. Harry Macklowe has a new, vacant building on 55th Street and might be willing to make a deal with Katz. I'm very friendly with Macklowe. I'd like to come up with an alternate deal to induce Ruben to back down" (*always have a Plan B*).

GREENWALD: "Okay. See what you can do."

Scene 4

Place: Ross's office where he prepares a checklist for his upcoming meeting with Macklowe. It looks like this.

 Questions needing answers:

1. Does Macklowe's building have at least 200,000 square feet of vacant space in 125 West 55th St.? Assume yes, but ask Macklowe.
2. What rent is Macklowe asking for his vacant space? What concessions are available such as free rent and money for tenant improvements? What lease term is available? Options available? Ask Macklowe but check ESG's database *(assume accuracy of information the other side gives you, but always verify it)*.
3. Who holds the mortgage on Macklowe's building *(is there a hidden negotiator)*?
4. What is Macklowe's financial condition? Assume it's good but verify.

 POST plans for Macklowe meeting:

P = Persons. Ross, Macklowe, and member of Macklowe's staff. Get name and function.

O = Objective. See if Macklowe has space to meet Katz's needs and if so on what terms is he willing to make a deal? *(creating the zone of uncertainty—staking out the starting negotiating positions of the two sides)*.

S = Strategy. Tell Macklowe that Katz is very strong financially and would be a great tenant to have in his building. Tell him that Katz has given me the authority to make a quick deal.

T = Tactics. Bring a history of Katz. Started in 1886 as the first advertising representative. Now #1 in New York. Have the financials of Katz available if necessary to verify net worth.

Ross calls Macklowe and arranges a meeting.

ACT 2

Scene 1

Place: Macklowe's office. Present are Macklowe, Ross, and Macklowe's CFO.

ROSS: "Hi, Harry. It's good to see you again (*creating a friendly atmosphere*). I'm here to bring you a first-rate tenant for 125 West 55th St. Have you got 175,000 square feet of vacant space?"

MACKLOWE: "Have I got 175,000 square feet? Hell, I've got a whole 550,000 square foot building vacant! What do you have in mind?"

ROSS: "I represent the Katz Agency which has 150,000 square feet at 1 Dag. They have a bunch of leases but I could convince them to move to 125 West 55th Street if I can get them a good deal. What are you asking in rent? How much free rent do you give? What's the value of the initial improvements you make for tenants?"

MACKLOWE: "My asking rent starts at $34 per square foot for lower floors and goes up for higher floors. I want $5.00 increases every five years. I'm looking for a minimum 10-year lease. I'll give a four-month free rent concession and I have a $30 per square foot work letter for tenant improvements. (*Ross has now established one parameter of the zone of uncertainty.*) But if you bring me the right tenant we'll work things out" (*voluntary useful admission*).

ROSS: "Okay, Harry. I hear you. Let me crunch some numbers and I'll get back to you."

Ross goes back to his office to have his accounting department (*using professionals*) compute the estimated cost to Katz of the proposed

Macklowe deal. Since Ross now has the parameters of Plan B, he sets up a new meeting with Ruben.

Scene 2

Place: Ruben's office. Present are Ruben, Ruben's son, and Ross.

ROSS: "Larry, I've been thinking over what you said and I agree that no one can make a better deal for the Katz Agency than you if you're willing to do so. They need a 10-year lease for 175,000 feet. What deal are you willing to make?"

RUBEN: "Here's what I'll do. I want them to increase the rent on the 75,000 square feet of cheap space to $36 per square foot starting immediately. On the rest of the space, I want $42 per square foot starting immediately. I want a bump of $4.00 per square foot every five years. I won't pay for any improvements to the space and there's no rent concession." (*Ross has now established the other parameter of the zone of uncertainty.*) "Go back and tell Katz that's my offer."

ROSS: "I'll discuss it with Katz and get back to you."

Ross goes back to his office to compare the Ruben proposal versus the Macklowe proposal.

Scene 3

Place: Ross's office. Ross and John Williams, a number cruncher at ESG, are present.

ROSS: "John, I asked you to run the numbers on Plan A (the Ruben deal) and Plan B (the Macklowe deal), did you do that?"

JOHN: "Yes. Here is the comparison."

	Deal	
	Ruben	**Macklowe**
Square footage:	175,000	175,000
Total rent (10 yrs.)	$12,300,000	$10,945,000
Tenant work	$3,750,000 (est.)	$3,750,000 (est.)
Cost of move	None	$1,000,000 (est.)
Broker's fee	$2,800,000	None (landlord pays)
Free rent	None	−$1,700,000
Loss on subletting existing space	None	$5,000,000 (est.)
Total cost (est.)	$18,850,000	$18,995,000

ROSS: "So the total cost of the Macklowe deal is $4,855,000 less than Ruben's offer if we eliminate the loss on the subletting of the existing space. Is that right?"

JOHN: "Yes. Also, I've assumed that Katz's share of any increases in taxes and operating expenses would be the same for both buildings."

ROSS: "Thanks, John. I'll relay this information to the Katz Agency."

Ross sets up meeting with Greenwald.

Scene 4

Place: Greenwald's office at the Katz Agency. Present are Ross, Greenwald, and Katz's CFO (Jones).

ROSS: "We've run the preliminary numbers on both deals, and while they look almost equal, a few things worry me. If we go the Macklowe route, the cost of your exposure on the Ruben space could be as much as $4 million. Your leases require you to pay that much in rents, whether you are in the building or not. Also, I'm not sure of how much money Katz will have to pay for improvements in the Macklowe building, beyond what Macklowe has provided. It could be a sizable expense. Since you shouldn't pay rent for both spaces at the same time, I'll have to get assurance that Macklowe can cover the remaining rent you owe at 1 Dag Plaza. Finally, I'm sure any deal will require his mortgage holder's approval, and I haven't started the hard bargaining yet so I'm not sure they'll okay the final deal I intend to make. I'd like your professionals to satisfy themselves on my estimates of all the costs involved."

GREENWALD: "Jones, please take care of that."

ROSS TO GREENWALD: "There are some intangibles for you to consider if you go the Macklowe route. You can't put a dollar value on them, but they should play a role in your final decision. Each floor in Macklowe's building is 30,000 square feet while the floors in Ruben's building are only 17,000 square feet. The larger floorplate means less traffic between floors and a more efficient operation. You'll need fewer copiers, fax machines, food pantries, and receptionists. These will substantially reduce operating costs. The location of the Macklowe building is better than Ruben's. It is more centrally located, close to transportation systems, and more prestigious. You can design a new space to suit your needs instead of trying to update space that is 15 years old. In making a long-term deal, price should not be your only consideration (*there's no right price for the wrong item*). Think it over and let me know how you would like to proceed."

For the next few months, Ross has meetings with Ruben, Macklowe, and the Katz people (*the invested time principle*). Cost estimates are obtained, financial projections are created, space designers and architects are consulted (*use of professionals*). Ross is unable to convince Ruben to be more reasonable in his demands. Macklowe is anxious to make a deal, but balks when discussing the need for him to make cash expenditures. The executive board of the Katz Agency (*find the decision makers*) convenes to decide what to do. Greenwald invites Ross to participate in the meeting.

FINAL ACT

Scene 1

Place: Greenwald's office after the heated board meeting. Present are Ross and Greenwald.

GREENWALD: "George, you heard the board. They're against spending money to solve a space problem that may occur in three years. They're gung ho for the merger that will cost us about $12 million and we'll have to borrow it from a bank. They're concerned that if we take on major expenditures, the bank won't make the loan. I think they're right.

"Unless you can pull a rabbit out of a hat, we'll sit tight and make a deal with Ruben for the additional space we need because of the merger. If we can't make a deal with him, we'll operate out of two locations. I hate not to take advantage of a market opportunity, but unless you can come up with a viable alternative, we'll pay you for your time and effort and call you in a few years."

ROSS: "I hear you loud and clear, but I still think I can rattle Ruben's cage so that he'll come up with a much fairer deal. I'd like to use Macklowe as leverage. There's no doubt that a deal with Ruben is the way to go if he's reasonable but there's a slim possibility that I can structure a deal with Macklowe that the board will approve—or even if they don't, I can use it as a wedge to get Ruben to lower his sights. Do I have your permission to try?"

GREENWALD: "Go to it and good luck, you'll need it."

Scene 2

Place: Ross goes back to his office to devise a plan to try to convince Macklowe to make a deal within the restrictions laid down by the Katz board (*necessary preplanning*). Before setting a meeting with Macklowe, Ross prepares a list of important questions (*making an agenda before a meeting*).

1. How can I make a deal with Macklowe where he advances all the money Katz needs for the move to Macklowe's building? Answer: Increase the rent to repay him.
2. How can I get Macklowe to take over the remaining obligations under the lease with Ruben? Answer: Quantify the exposure and blend it into the rent.
3. What assurance do I have that Macklowe will meet his monetary obligations? Answer: Insist on money up front as a condition of signing the lease.
4. I've been told that a major law firm has been negotiating to take a big block of space in Macklowe's building but the deal has stalled, why? Answer: Ask Macklowe or the head of the law firm or both.
5. I'm going to ask for a low rent and huge monetary concessions from Macklowe and I know the approval of Macklowe's mortgage holder will be required. How can I convince them to approve the deal? Answer: Convince them a building with a less than ideal lease is better than sitting with an empty building at a time when tenants are scarce.
6. Does Macklowe know I'm trying to make a deal with Ruben? Answer: Assume he does but try to juggle both deals.
7. How can I script this negotiation? Answer: You can't; there are too many variables. Just wing it.
8. What do I do if Ruben learns I'm dealing with Macklowe? Answer: Tell him that it is because his deal is outrageous and if he's reasonable I'll make a deal with him.

After carefully devising the answers to the questions Macklowe will probably raise, Ross sets a meeting with Macklowe. Ross tells him the Katz Agency is ready to make a deal and Ross thinks, although it's a highly unusual deal, perhaps he can convince Macklowe it's a good one even though he knows initially he won't like it. (*Aim high and you'll come out better.*)

Scene 3

Place: Macklowe's office. Present are Ross, Macklowe, Macklowe's CFO, and Macklowe's lawyer.

ROSS TO MACKLOWE: "Harry, I've gotten the Katz Agency to carefully consider taking a lease in your building, but it will require several millions of dollars of up front money from you."

MACKLOWE: "George, to tell you the truth since the building's been vacant so long, I haven't made any payments on my mortgage. If the lender wanted to, it could foreclose and own the building outright. The lender has agreed to give me an opportunity to salvage my investment by finding a deal they will approve." (*Ross just uncovered a hidden decision maker.*) "Any money you need to make the Katz deal must come from the lender. I can negotiate a deal and recommend it, but that's as far as I can go."

ROSS: "Let me outline the deal I think Katz will accept, hear me out, and let's put our heads together to figure a way to induce your mortgagee to accept it. Here are the basic terms that Katz wants; I'll give you the bad news first:

1. Once Katz makes a deal with you, they want to be free of all financial obligations from the space covered by any Ruben lease. You'll have to assume all of their monetary obligations under their leases. That means you'll have to quantify in your own mind the dollar value of Katz's exposure, taking into account

the amount you think you can save by subletting or getting a release from Ruben. Then you'd have to agree to pay it when due, and recoup it by increasing your rent.

2. Katz's architects figure that the installation Katz will make in your building will cost $8,750,000 more than your building standard. That excess will have to be funded by you, but can also be recouped by increasing the rent.

3. To be consistent with what is presently available in the marketplace, the basic rent must be $10 per square foot below your asking rent.

4. Katz needs $12 million to complete its merger and wants to borrow the money from you and repay it with interest over the term of the lease.

Now for the good news:

1. Katz is a financially solid entity that has been in business since 1886. They are an excellent credit risk.

2. Katz is willing to sign a 15-year lease on space on the lower floors, which are the hardest for you to rent. This will enable you to make the deal you have been trying to make with the law firm for the upper floors. Between the two leases, the building will be almost 100% rented in a depressed market.

3. If I get the green light, I can finish the deal with you within one week which means less lost time for you.

4. Using my relationships with your mortgage holder (*the importance of building relationships*), I think together we can convince them that increasing the amount of the mortgage by the money you need and having a 100% rented building is a much better position for the mortgagee than having a smaller mortgage on an empty building during a real estate recession of unknown duration."

MACKLOWE'S ATTORNEY: "There's no way that Ruben will consent to an assignment or cancellation of the leases in the Ruben building. How can Macklowe get the benefits of any subletting of that space?"

ROSS: "The Katz Agency and Macklowe could sign a takeover agreement whereby Macklowe is responsible for the rent Katz is obligated to pay under the Ruben lease. Katz would agree to make any sublease of the Ruben space that Macklowe requests. The takeover agreement will be structured in such a way to protect Macklowe and Katz from a default by either of them."

MACKLOWE TO ROSS: "That's the wackiest deal I ever heard of."

ROSS TO MACKLOWE: "I agree it's unusual but I don't think it's wacky. What's your alternative? Is it better to sit with a vacant building and lose it to your mortgage lender?"

MACKLOWE TO HIS ATTORNEY: "George has a point there. Draw up the papers and let's see if we can make the deal work."

MACKLOWE TO ROSS: "One thing I need from you. If I go through all these gymnastics and agree to make a deal, I want your promise that you won't go back to Ruben and make a deal with him."

ROSS: "Once the paperwork has reached the level that I feel comfortable that we have a deal, I'll stop negotiating with Ruben. However, until that point I still consider myself free to negotiate with Ruben" (*create an incentive to move quickly*).

Ross, together with the Katz representatives, spend about three intensive weeks negotiating the documents containing the terms set out by Ross and verbally approved by Macklowe. When the deal has reached the stage that Ross believes it will happen. Ross sets another meeting with Ruben.

Scene 4

Place: Ruben's office. Present are Ross, Ruben, and Ruben's son.

ROSS: "Larry, up to now you've refused to budge from your prior negotiating position. As a courtesy (*maintaining a relationship*), I'm here to give you one more chance to change your mind or you'll lose Katz as a tenant."

Ross then tells Ruben the terms of the deal that Macklowe is willing to make with Katz.

RUBEN TO ROSS: "I don't believe that Macklowe will honor any deal he makes, he hasn't got the money to do so."

ROSS: "Larry, you've known me for a long time; if I say it can be done, then it can be done. If you doubt it just stick to your position and watch what happens" (*take it or leave it*).

RUBEN TO ROSS: "I don't care what you say; you'll never make that deal with Macklowe."

Ross leaves Ruben's office and calls Macklowe and says, "Harry, if you put our deal to bed I promise you I'm through negotiating with Ruben."

Macklowe's deal with Katz is finalized and approved by Macklowe's mortgage holder. Ross tells Greenwald to call a meeting of the board of directors of the Katz Agency to approve the Macklowe deal. Greenwald calls the meeting and Ross explains the advantages of the Macklowe deal:

1. Katz gets the $12 million it needs to complete the merger and pays it back as part of the rent under its lease with Macklowe.
2. Katz gets brand new space in a new, prestigious midtown office building.
3. Katz is protected from its exposure under the leases with Ruben.
4. The larger floor size of the Macklowe building creates greater efficiency and a savings in the cost of operations of more than $1 million per year.

The Katz board approves the Macklowe deal. However, Ruben has a mole on the Katz board and learns of the approval of the Macklowe deal. Ruben calls Ross.

RUBEN TO ROSS: "George, I'm willing to beat the Macklowe deal. Let's meet and work it out."

ROSS TO RUBEN: "Larry, you had your chance and you said I couldn't do what I said I could do. Now the ship has sailed and you're not on board. Sorry, I gave my word to Macklowe that if he honored his deal with me, I was through negotiating with you. (*Keep your commitments.*) Maybe next time you won't doubt my word."

THE END

17

Six Tactics for Increasing Your Power in a Negotiation

T HE RECURRING THEME in Trump-style negotiation is looking for ways to satisfy both sides, to structure a deal so that everyone feels that he or she comes out a winner. I experienced an unusual example of this type of a negotiation approach when I worked for Sol Goldman and Alex DiLorenzo Jr. in the 1960s. One day an elderly, disheveled broker came into our offices and handed me a listing for an apartment building in Brooklyn Heights. It was for sale by a family who had built it 40 years before and owned it ever since. The asking price was $860,000. Not knowing whether it might be of interest to Sol Goldman, I showed him the listing. Sol knew all about the property and had tried to buy it years ago but was unsuccessful. He told me he would love to buy the property and when I told him the asking price he was shocked because it was so low. He told me to find out how many people the broker had already shown the listing to. So I spoke to the broker again, who told me we were the only real estate investors he'd come to, because we were well known as the number one buyer of Brooklyn properties.

When I told Goldman that, he said, "George, if this deal gets out in the market, there will be a bidding war for it. We have to avoid one and move quickly. Tell the broker I'll buy the property for $1 million." I said, "Sol, they're only asking $860,000 how can I justify $1 million?" He told me, "Hey, you're the lawyer, you figure it out."

I went back to the broker, who was still sitting in my office, and said, "My client likes the property, but there's a major problem. The price is too low." The broker didn't understand what I said and he replied, "Well, I know they're asking $860,000 but I think they might sell it for $800,000." "You weren't listening to me," I told him, "The price is too low, if you raise the price to $1 million you've got a deal. Just bring me a contract for that price and I'll give you a check for $100,000 as a down payment and we'll close in 30 days." The broker was thoroughly confused and asked me, "Why would anyone pay $1 million for something they could buy for $860,000?" Reaching for a plausible explanation I said, "My client is an eccentric millionaire and he won't buy anything costing less than $1 million. That's his style. As I told you, if you come back to me with a contract for $1 million, I'm authorized to sign it and give you the down payment."

The broker left my office like a shot and came back the next day with a contract, which I signed, and gave him the $100,000 deposit. Now, the kicker was that before title passed, Goldman had lined up a nonrecourse first mortgage on the property for $1.4 million from a bank—the bank thought it was worth at least that amount. Goldman took title with his own money and a few months later I closed the loan with the bank without disclosing the original purchase price. By overpaying Goldman had ensured that he would get the property quickly. With his instinct, he believed he knew the property's true value, and he was right; he made a great deal.

If you approach negotiation with the idea that one side must win and the other must lose, you're not using Trump-style negotiation. Your goal is not to squeeze everything you can out of the other side, but to create a deal they can live with. Both sides in this transaction got more than they were willing to accept, and both walked away feeling like winners. Whenever you can create that feeling, you are executing a Trump-style negotiation.

With skill, creativity, and showmanship, you can turn adversaries into allies by showing them how it is possible to make a deal acceptable to both sides. The desired outcome is mutual satisfaction.

The last step in explaining how Trump-style negotiation works is to summarize six of the most important deal-making techniques you can use. Mastering these basic fundamentals will guarantee you a higher success rate in closing mutually satisfying negotiations:

1. *Keep exceptional records.* Remember what I said earlier: The side that is more prepared in any negotiation has a better chance of winning. The notes you take during a negotiation serve as a defense against the other side raising new issues or contradicting themselves later. If you are able to refer to a specific discussion, including the date and what was said, you have a compelling argument.

2. *Wherever possible develop your own forms and create the aura of legitimacy.* It is a truism that the side that prepares documents decides what goes in and what stays out. The aura of legitimacy is set by you presenting something for signature and authenticating it by saying something like, "This is what I used in a similar deal with GM, if they approved it, it should be fine with you." The existence of a contract, application, agreement, or other document carries the aura of legitimacy merely because it exists and people have a tendency to believe the written word.

3. *If you can, use company policy as a negotiating tool.* If you represent a company in your negotiations, simply presenting the argument that "That is our company's policy" will put an end to many arguments. Somehow company policy is like a mandate from God. The other side is likely to realize there's no point in trying to change something as inflexible as company policy. They rarely probe to find out whether or not the policy, in fact, exists or *is* that inflexible.

4. *Be willing to take calculated risks.* You have to play to win. Taking risks may be reckless if you have not evaluated the risk and reward beforehand. But a *calculated* risk is worth taking if you are

willing and able to live with the consequences. For example, if someone wants to delay the final stages of a negotiation, you can calculate that the other side has more to lose than you do by walking away. So it might be worth the risk of saying, "This is my best offer. Take it or leave it." Successful negotiators are willing to take calculated risks. Suppose, for example, I make you the following offer, "I've tossed this quarter 49 times and it always came up heads. I'm willing to give you 100 to 1 odds that it will come up heads the 50th time as well." Now you know the odds are 50-50 so you would jump at the opportunity, right? Let's change the scenario a bit. Assume that your total life savings is $200,000 and I say, "I'll bet $20 million against your $200,000 that it will be heads again." The odds haven't changed, but the stakes have, and suddenly the possibility of losing everything becomes a reality. You begin to think, "With my luck it'll come up heads again, and I'll be wiped out." You refuse the bet even though it was a well-calculated risk. Any negotiator who has the courage to take risks has an advantage over those who lack the courage to do so.

5. *Use time as the ultimate negotiating weapon*. Every negotiation has a time element involved in various phases of its development. As long as you are not forced to operate under a deadline governing your side, you can use time as a weapon to control the negotiation. When you are aware that the other side *must* end the discussion within a specific time and place, don't begin negotiating in earnest until the latest possible moment because that's when the other side is most vulnerable to accepting your suggestions.

You can also make effective use of delay as long as it furthers your agenda or makes the other side eventually come around to an agreement because they get tired of waiting. Deadlines, delays, and deadlocks are all time-related methods of negotiation. Figure out how to use each of these at appropriate times to enhance your negotiating power, and by all means avoid allowing the other side to use time against you.

6. *Make and use general commitments to gain concessions.* You can make promises to the other side of a general nature, to gain the advantage. For example, you can say, "I promise that I'm going to see this through until we reach an agreement." This is a moral commitment to not walk away. But if you are going to make such a commitment, you should expect reciprocity. Keep in mind that you can choose to refute your moral commitment if circumstances so require, but if the other side does so you can remind them of their agreement and get them to continue negotiating.

* * *

The entire field of negotiation is merely the continual use of diverse methods to communicate ideas that will achieve a favorable result. Some people are effective motivators and others are not. Some hold their cards close to their vest and carefully control what they do, say, or employ to impress others. Inept negotiators signal when they have a good hand, or a poor hand, by what they say, write, or the actions they take. Skilled negotiators are easy to deal with, but they get what they want.

Your awareness of negotiation skills and tactics is essential to making the process work. You certainly don't want to find yourself in a situation where you're at a disadvantage; and if you do, find a way to delay the proceedings until you've had a chance to create a plan that can reverse that situation. In this book, I have provided you with a series of strategies, tactics, and skills worth mastering. Anyone who studies the philosophy of Trump-style negotiation will eventually be able to apply these skills in his or her own negotiations with other people. I never said it would be easy, but over time you will create your own data bank of what worked and what didn't.

The ability to negotiate effectively is a worthwhile talent in any situation, industry, or organization. You will discover that it transcends your professional life and carries over into your personal life as well. You will be better equipped to deal with salespeople, friends, spouses, and children once you gain the insights into what people are really thinking when they say something. You will be much better equipped to be an effective salesperson because that's what a skilled negotiator is. Once you are able to recognize common errors or human nature, you will be a much better negotiator on every level.

You're always negotiating. It never stops. Just remember this most important element of Trump-style negotiation: You can only achieve mutual satisfaction and complete the biggest and best deals when you build a relationship of trust and rapport with those with whom you become involved.

INDEX

importance of, 4–5, 259
nature of, 11–12
nonverbal forms of, 5–6
planning, 75–76
rules of, 3–4
truth in, xv–xvi
what it is not, 10–12
New Jersey Casino Control
    Commission, 20–21
Newspapers, and aura of
    legitimacy, 88
New York City, in Commodore
    Hotel negotiations, 53–54,
    63–64
New York Real Estate Board, 41
New York State Urban
    Development Corporation,
    53–54
New York University's School of
    Continuing Education and
    Professional Studies,
    xviii–xix
Nibbling tactic, 158–159
Nonverbal negotiation, 5–6
Notes, 147, 213, 221, 256
Note takers, 143
No-trust discount, 29–30

O

Objectives, in POST technique,
    141–142, 145
Office lease forms, 41
"One good turn deserves
    another" tactic, 93–94, 123
112 Central Park South
    negotiations, 85–86

Optimists, 2, 36
Other side:
    building up negotiator's
        stature with, 179
    constraints of, 44
    finding common ground with,
        26–27
    identifying key people on,
        42–44
    learning about, 44–45
    motivations of, 44
    researching, 133–134
    soliciting help from, 177
    understanding needs of, 28–29
    weaknesses of, 44–48
Outside date, 73–74

P

Pace, controlling, 66–81. *See also*
    Time
    critical path, 73–74
    deadlines, 70–73
    deadlocks, 77–81
    delays, 75, 257
    guidelines, 69–70
    importance of, 67–69
    Murphy's Law, 77
    parallel negotiating tracks, 76
    planning negotiation, 75–76
    as power negotiating tactic,
        159–161
Palm Beach zoning board, 197,
    203–204
Palmieri, Victor, 56–57
Parallel negotiating tracks, 76
Patience, 178–179, 191–192